COMRADES, NOT FRIENDS

THE REVOLUTIONARY FRONT, ANTIFASCISM, AND CLASS STRUGGLE

Emma Hagberg

Translated by Gabriel Kuhn

Foreword by Tomas Rothaus

WCH

PM

Comrades, Not Friends: The Revolutionary Front, Antifascism, and Class Struggle
Emma Hagberg

ISBN: 979-8-88744-019-4 (paperback)
ISBN: 979-8-88744-198-6 (ebook)
Library of Congress Control Number: 2026932807

Cover design by John Yates / stealworks.com
Interior design by briandesign

10 9 8 7 6 5 4 3 2 1

PM Press
PO Box 23912
Oakland, CA 94623
www.pmpress.org

Printed in the USA.

For Dennis

CONTENTS

FOREWORD

Tomas Rothaus

"Nazis are for hunting."

I no longer remember if we said it to them, or if they said it to us. But it was clearly the joint mentality of our improvised little antifascist gang.

It's a December night in 2005, the eve of the annual Salem March, an event in a suburb of Stockholm that has become one of the largest annual mobilizations of European fascists. The city is crawling with Nazis.

What belongs together more often than not comes together, and so it is not too surprising that this particular group of antifascists—a mix of Revolutionary Front (RF) and Antifascist Action (AFA) Stockholm on the Swedish side (we weren't altogether clear as to who was who, and we weren't in the habit of asking too many unnecessary questions), and some comrades from a well-established autonomous antifa group from Göttingen, Germany, which shall not be named—are sitting around a table at some unremarkable central Stockholm bar, waiting anxiously for the phone call that will spring us into action.

Some of us first met in Gothenburg during the EU Summit of 2001. In October 2005, we turned an attempted Nazi demonstration in Göttingen into what became known as "Disaster Day for Cops and Nazis," erecting dozens of flaming barricades and putting hundreds of Nazis and the two thousand cops protecting them on the run. Now the comrades from Stockholm had invited us to their city as part of a yearslong antifascist cultural and militant exchange program.

Finally, the phone rings. Words are exchanged in Elvish, incomprehensible to us, but my recollections are pure nostalgia for the quintessential Nazi-hunting experience: the quick exit, the hurried and determined pace, the adrenaline and anxiety of imminent combat. A small mob of North Face jackets (which we were for some reason stupidly fanatical about) and Adidas tracksuits trying to make its way through the city as discreetly as possible.

We and RF cultivated a "whole and clean" style distinct from the autonomous left, an advantage when faced by cops and, especially, fascists. Not only did we see the latter when they didn't see us, but in the case of many an unfortunate nationalist, they mistook us for friendlies.

Eventually, the target comes into view, and we break into a run in a flurry of ski masks and leather gloves. It's a group of Nazis who've been spotted drinking at a bar in a trendy shopping area of Stockholm, and our telephone spotter opens the doors for us on arrival.

The scene was almost comical, cementing in my head the notion that Sweden was in fact a lawless "Never-Neverland Wild West for Antifas," in which we could apparently do whatever, whenever it pleased us—a perspective I was always concerned might offend Swedish militants, only to read in this book that many of them apparently shared the assessment, stating that well into the 2010s, "you had to be really stupid or really unlucky to get arrested."

It's over as quickly as it started, and the Nazis are thoroughly routed. Nazis are bullies; they aren't used to being hunted. I recall the fear in their eyes as they crouched down, trying to protect themselves from the hail of glass. We made sure they knew it was militant antifascists who had blessed them with this experience, and within seconds we had vanished.

What I've described could be a snapshot of just about any militant antifascist crew's praxis. But comrades from the Revolutionary Front would take this a step further. They boldly used such actions to make propaganda videos, which were well produced and appealing (with clean graphics and upbeat music) and expressed their understanding of militant antifascism: that Nazis are for hunting, that they should be safe nowhere, and that antifascists should not hesitate to go on the offensive.

For years, Revfront Media produced video after video, garnering tens of thousands of views on YouTube and other channels. The videos featured increasingly daring actions by its members: Nazis beaten in broad daylight in city centers, determined antifascist mobs descending on Nazi meeting places, and the notorious home visits, in which masked antifascists would enter the homes of fascists, in one case literally taking an axe to the door, destroying everything in their wake. The videos inspired those in our camp and terrorized those who saw themselves as the next potential victim. They usually closed with graphic animations laying out in simple terms the orientation and priorities of the group: "Internationalism. Socialism. Antifascism. Workers' Rights. Women's Struggle. Class Struggle."

RF was unabashedly combative, nothing if not audacious, and refreshingly simple in the clarity with which the group communicated its objectives. At a time when many antifascists were deeply frustrated with the often insular, hyperintellectual, and largely student and middle-class character of autonomous antifascism, RF differentiated itself—in a vein perhaps reminiscent of Class War or Red Action in the United Kingdom of the 1990s—by firmly placing itself in the context not only of revolutionary antifascism but of combating the far right as *workers*, in the interests of the working class pursuing socialism.

As a Latin American anarchist and antifascist who, in the 2000s, suffered through a decade-long stint in German antifascism—rich in tradition and large in numbers but to me often wholly foreign—I understood more about RF while reading through this book than I was able to grasp during the heat of common actions. A lot of things, which I had felt instinctively but never analyzed intellectually, became clear to me. Our visits to Sweden and the interactions with the antifa crews were a welcome—for me, almost existential—breath of fresh air. As I went through the interviews in this book, it became clear that there were numerous reasons for this. We shared similar frustrations. For example: Was the emphasis on "research and surveillance" of Nazis in the antifascist scene—"research for research's sake"—a way for middle-class activists unwilling to put themselves in danger to feel good about themselves? What was the use of exposing Nazis if it didn't lead to concrete consequences?

We thought a lot about whether the antifascist scene was effective. Were we indeed hindering or stopping fascist activity? How did we present ourselves outwardly? Did every mobilization really need a five-page call that was barely understandable to me as a foreign-born anarchist, let alone a regular person on the street? Were we not alienating people with our intellectualism, our insular language, and our scenester ghetto behavior? As revolutionary antifascists, our goal must not be simply opposition to fascism but working toward a liberated society, in which the conditions that breed fascism are a thing of the past. But how do we build a movement when we are wholly incapable of communicating with society at large?

We probably also shared some shortcomings. We were impulsive and visceral. It is questionable whether a revolutionary militant should really risk life and liberty to confront any random fascist they encounter, no matter the place, the time, or the odds. And while we rejected the codes of the autonomous antifa scene, weren't we just a different version of the same problem? We, too, had our unspoken dress codes. We often had less-than-stellar gender ratios. And we clearly attracted a demographic that, for one reason or another, carried with it a certain proneness to violence.

But not every organization necessarily needs to be for everybody. What's important is that RF filled a void that allowed people who didn't feel comfortable within the structures of the autonomous and antifascist left but who identified with militant antifascism and revolutionary ideas to find a political home. Cultivating visceral hatred for Nazis and instinctive identification with left-wing politics among working-class youth is essential to depriving fascists of fertile ground to recruit and organize. As a militant who spent years in cities where Nazis once dominated the streets but were eventually beaten back by a combination of the uncompromising violence of militant antifascists together with a broader political and cultural front, I can't stress enough the importance of this. When alternative youth, marginalized people, and just about anybody who doesn't fit into the worldview of Nazis has to constantly be on the defensive, nothing else can flourish. RF recognized this and did a stellar job of "chasing the Nazis into the shadows." Reading through the interviews in this book, it seemed that, as central as violence and militance were to achieving this, so was RF's ability to mobilize less overtly political social groups. This is likely due to the audacity of its actions and its reputation, but just as much to the aesthetic it cultivated and to its organizing as a disciplined cadre organization. In many regards, it was recognizable on the street level as, essentially, a hyperpoliticized youth gang.

RF existed where the lines between cultural and political antifascism get blurry. As members themselves assert, this often leads to interpersonal relationships more characteristic of street gangs or soldiers having experienced combat together than your classic political organization. Affinity strengthened through battle doesn't necessarily depend on close political alignment. Those who put their lives and freedom on the line next to me are my brothers and sisters, even if we disagree on some political points. Of course, placing proximity through danger and adrenaline above political cohesion is problematic and a double-edged sword. But the interviews in this book show that former RF members are aware of this and reflect on it openly and self-critically. They approach other potential pitfalls of violent and adrenaline-filled politics in a similar manner: issues of addiction and abuse, of personal trauma, and of normalizing violence outside of politics.

Eventually, RF encountered situations that forced it to question the sustainability of its political project. The terrain it was operating in began to shift, and the state became a more significant actor in the antifas-versus-fascists equation. The one question I had often asked myself with regard to RF—"How are these people not in prison?"—was about to be answered: They would be.

RF may now be a thing of the past, but there is a deep and lasting political relevance to collective experiences of militant antifascism such as its members shared, not least given the current wave of fascist and authoritarian movements we find ourselves battling. Rescuing relevant collective experiences is extremely important, especially when, as in this case, the protagonists are allowed to speak in their own words instead of having their story told by academics and pundits seeking to psychologize their actions or place them on a scale of political extremism.

As former RF members declare in this book, times have changed. Today, there are cameras everywhere. Fascism and fascist ideas are packaged for the mainstream. Methods that worked years ago no longer do. Yet it remains easy to identify with the motivations of RF and be impressed by their audacity. We may have to adapt the methods to our times and places, but the driving force will always be the same. If it is considered "extreme" to proclaim loudly and boldly that the enduring antidote to fascism is class consciousness, workers' power, and socialism, it's a badge we can wear with pride.

In the spirit of this book, I'll close by letting the comrades speak in their own words, quoting from their notorious appearance in a 2014 VICE News report titled "The Rise of Sweden's Far-Left Militants":

> The working class built this society. Every house you see, every road you see, the working class built it. And still we've got nothing to say about how this society is going to progress. So if the same society that pisses on me on an everyday basis calls me a terrorist, then I'm feeling kind of proud, actually.

TRANSLATOR'S PREFACE TO THE ENGLISH EDITION

The book at hand appeared in Swedish in the fall of 2024 under the title *18.6—Kamrater, inte vänner*. The numbers 18 and 6 are references to the positions in the alphabet of the letters *R* and *F*: Revolutionära Fronten. Within the autonomous left in Sweden, the organization is commonly referred to as RF, on occasion as 18. The subtitle of the Swedish edition translates as "Comrades, Not Friends." The meaning will become clear in the course of the book.

The Revolutionary Front was founded in 2001 and dissolved in 2015. No other group within the autonomous left in Sweden ever received as much attention. Within Sweden's left, RF was highly controversial. One reason was the organization's militancy (unparalleled in Swedish history), another the disdain that RF held for the norms and standards of the leftist scene.

The militancy also drew the attention of mainstream media, which reported about the organization regularly, especially during its final years. Programs about RF were aired on Swedish TV during prime time. There was also international coverage. A VICE News program on RF was viewed by millions of people. Connections to the Swedish hip-hop scene led to RF being featured in music videos of popular artists such as Kartellen. The videos that the organization itself uploaded about its actions were viewed online by hundreds of thousands of people.

RF's dissolution was preceded by a wave of repression, which led to several (active and no longer active) members receiving prison sentences between fourteen months and six and a half years. An additional number of members received suspended sentences. SÄPO, the Swedish security service, regularly listed RF as a domestic threat in its reports. Meanwhile, the Left Party expelled members who expressed sympathy with the organization.

This book tells the story of RF from the perspective of its members. The author, Emma Hagberg, pulls their voices together, adding only modest commentary. The book's core consists of interviews with former members and written memories. It also contains articles from the RF website, www.revfront.org, as well as photographs, banners, and flyers.[1]

In the contributions to the book, pride over what RF has achieved is blended with self-critique. Internal tensions are not swept under the rug.

The reception of the book in Sweden has proven that RF remains controversial. Some commentators felt that the problematic aspects of the organization don't receive enough room, while others think that inner-left conflicts, especially with the network Antifascist Action (AFA), receive too much. The fact is that there is no comparable documentary study of RF. The fact is also that RF was one of the most important antifascist, working-class organizations in Europe of the early twenty-first century. RF's significance reaches far beyond the borders of Sweden. The questions raised by the organization about militancy, class politics, antifascism, political organizing, and revolutionary orientation are universal.

The notes in the translation have been adapted to an English audience.

I thank the author, the designer, and PM Press for their great collaboration!

INTRODUCTION

Myths surrounded the Revolutionary Front already during its existence. Lots of people had opinions. The media focused on the violence, the trials, and the prison sentences. They liked to present individual members as leaders and compared RF to fascist organizations. Also, the Swedish security service, SÄPO (Säkerhetspolisen), focused on the violence and declared RF a threat to Swedish democracy. They, too, suggested that RF could be compared to fascist groups.

RF was also criticized within the autonomous left.[1] RF was accused of machismo and recklessness, and certainly not considered "politically correct." The criticism was partly a reaction to RF accusing the rest of the autonomous left of elitism. It considered the autonomous scene as a subculture, not a political movement.

The way that RF has been portrayed from the outside is well known. This book will portray the organization in a different way. It is based on the stories of the members themselves. RF was characterized by a strong collective identity, unprecedented within the Swedish left. This makes it unique.

RF members never talked to the media, with two exceptions.[2] The organization communicated almost exclusively through its own channels. The material gathered for this book is the first of its kind.

RF formed in 2001 and dissolved in 2015. I interviewed thirty people for this book, some of them more than once. The interviews were conducted in 2022 and 2023. Over a much longer period of time, I have had many informal conversations with former RF members. None of the people I interviewed wanted to see their name in print. I have also gone through RF lectures and articles as well as internal documents such as minutes from meetings.

The book is structured chronologically, starting with the founding of the organization and ending with its dissolution. RF's history is divided into four parts, following rough time frames, although the boundaries are sometimes blurry. Written memories help capture the historical moment in which the organization was active. The book has twelve chapters, each one dedicated to a particular topic.

To present all interviews in full length would not have been possible within this publication. But all voices are included. Without them, there would be no book!

Political activism never occurs in a vacuum; it is always a reaction to social conditions. RF, too, is a reaction to the social conditions in which its members were fostered. Most of them grew up in the 1990s. At the time, Sweden went through an economic crisis, the unemployment rate reached unprecedented heights, and neoliberalism established itself. Therefore, not only is the history of RF an account of a militant socialist organization, but it also provides insights into the political circumstances of the time.

It is important to remember that RF was a reaction to the state of the autonomous left in Sweden. Without acknowledging the complicated relationship between RF and the rest of the autonomous left, RF cannot be understood.

2000-2005

THE BEGINNINGS

"

In the early 2000s, it was not at all unusual to encounter Nazis in Gothenburg or Örebro who wore their convictions on their sleeves. Literally! The National Socialist Front was quite big, even though, in Örebro, no one was really interested in a political party. There, most Nazis were still skinheads beating up foreigners.

"We Were Young, We Wanted Action!"

When the Revolutionary Front appeared on the political scene, the organization distanced itself consciously from the autonomous left, which members felt was dominated by middle-class folks. Alongside the uncompromising struggle against fascism on the streets, this gave RF a special place within the left.

Around the year 2000, a few people who had come of age in Gothenburg and Örebro during the 1990s began to discuss the foundation of a new political group. They felt that the autonomous left was characterized by elitism, rejecting everyone who didn't fit into the scene. Some of the RF founders had been active in the autonomous left themselves. They say that they repeatedly observed people being ostracized because they didn't live up to the scene's norms and expectations. The RF founders found it difficult to bring childhood friends to political events, since they were rejected because of their background, their conduct, or merely their clothes. The founders also criticized the autonomous left for talking too much and doing too little.

In the following interview, an RF founding member talks about, among other things, the connections of the earliest RF members to the football supporter scene:

> Some of us were active in the autonomous left, others in the Revolutionary Communist Youth, the Young Left, the Syndicalist Youth League (SUF), or in Antifascist Action (AFA).[1] But the left subculture was very insular. Our friends from the suburbs had no place in it.[2] They didn't fit. Once, I brought some of them along to an event, but all they said was, "Hey, who are these weirdos?" That was it, they never felt like returning. Besides, there was too little action. We were always told, "You can't just give the Nazis a hiding, you need to have a plan and think long-term!" That's not entirely wrong, I suppose, but we were simply too impatient. People in the autonomous left liked to talk, but they didn't do anything. We were young, we wanted action! What we got instead was too much lifestyle, too much university, too much morality, and way too little action.
>
> ***What distinguished RF from AFA? AFA was an established antifascist network.***
> We were able to recruit kids from the suburbs, kids who liked football. AFA had no connection to these people. For us, AFA was part of the autonomous subculture. Their members came from other leftist groups such as SUF. It might have been different elsewhere, but in Gothenburg they were very insular. Some of us were AFA members before we founded RF and always remained friendly with AFA. But experiences with AFA differed from member to member. In the beginning, we sometimes still worked with them, but there was no continuous collaboration. On a personal level, there were no major problems.
>
> ***What was the relationship like to the rest of the autonomous left? How did other leftists perceive you?***

There was no official collaboration, only personal contacts. On occasion, we would do things with other groups, but in general we kept our distance, since we didn't want to be part of the leftist swamp. You couldn't always draw ironclad boundaries, but we wanted to speak to people outside of the political scene and do our own thing.

How did other leftists perceive us? In the beginning, they didn't take us seriously. Some predicted that we wouldn't last for more than six months. But there were always people who had a different perspective and who we were friendly with.

The events around the 2001 EU summit in Gothenburg had a strong impact on the autonomous left in Sweden.[3] They might not have destroyed the scene entirely, but it was seriously shaken up. Much energy went into supporting people standing trial and ending up in prison. But the forms of political activism didn't change much. It was still Reclaim the Streets and stuff like that, even though it was obvious that this no longer brought results. In my opinion, the autonomous left clung to forms of activism whose time was up, while the scene was shrinking.

What was the fascist movement like at the time?

It was much more present on the streets than today. In the early 2000s, it was not at all unusual to encounter Nazis in Gothenburg or Örebro who wore their convictions on their sleeves. Literally! The National Socialist Front (NSF)[4] was quite big, even though, in Örebro, no one was really interested in a political party. There, most Nazis were still skinheads beating up foreigners.

We weren't many in RF in the beginning, but we knew how to fight. For a political group in Sweden, we had plenty of experience with violence. We could enter a fight a few men short and still win. A big group doesn't help when most people just get in the way. In that case, they are only a security risk.

Our credo was that the Nazis must never feel safe, even

when we're outnumbered. Six against ten? No problem, we'll attack nonetheless!

Were there any groups before RF that attacked fascists in the same way?
AFA did attack, but it was different. Whenever we visited an AFA group to do an action with them, it was us taking the initiative. Not all AFA groups were the same, but for us, everyone else was only doing things half-heartedly.

When did RF make its first official appearance?
On May 1, 2002, in Gothenburg. That day, we presented our name with a banner and everything. We painted the banner at a friend's apartment the night before, on Walpurgis Night.

Do you still have the banner?
No, it disappeared during an anti-Nazi demo when things got a bit hectic.

Weren't you mainly a circle of friends in the beginning? Did you have a strategy for your street activism?
Yes, we were a circle of friends. With the founding of the organization, everything became a little more formal, but in general we were a bunch of people who had already hung out before. We spent a lot of time together. The borders between hanging out and political work were never clearly drawn during the early years.

Did we have a strategy? We wanted to chase the Nazis out of the streets, and we wanted them to no longer appear tough and cool. They were often perceived as such, especially among middle-class kids and in smaller towns. We figured that they'd appear less cool with black eyes and their teeth knocked in. We knew that it would be hard to get rid of some of them, but we reckoned that kids on the margins of the Nazi scene might have second thoughts because of our attacks.

Eventually, RF grew, and our circle of friends turned into a bigger group. But still, during the early years, we knew most newcomers personally. Many were active football hooligans, particularly in support of GAIS but also IFK.[5]

What role did GAIS play for RF?

It's a little complicated. The RF founders were GAIS supporters. When we first put up our website, it even included a link to the club. That wasn't based on a collective decision, though, it was more of a joke by the person who built the website. I reckon he needed stuff to fill it with. In any case, we also wanted to send a message with the reference to football. The left looked down on football, and we wanted to be different.

But then, our very first new member was an IFK supporter! Later we had supporters from a variety of clubs, also Örgryte.[6] And the selection became even more diverse when RF expanded to Stockholm.

The significance of GAIS dwindled during RF's history, but it was almost the most popular club within RF. Football remained important for the organization throughout, not least for the recruitment of new members, but also when it came to social events. The overlap between football and politics was nothing new, of course. It all started in the 1980s. We managed to recruit many people there, people who were too political for the hooligan firms but not welcome in most leftist groups, who just saw them as dumb jocks.

MEMORY "NORMALITY WAS OUR MASK."

"An example from the early times: It was a summer day in 2002, around noon, and six of us were out looking for Nazis. Some of us carried improvised weapons. I had prepared the inside pocket of my jacket so that it allowed me to carry an iron bar. We also had telescopic batons and wooden clubs with us, and one person had pocketed a screwdriver.

We saw eight or nine Nazis in a park in the inner city. We observed them for a while. It seemed that they were only out socializing; one of them carried a bunch of six-packs.

We made our move just as they were boarding a tram. We attacked with groups from two sides and pulled no punches. The Nazis were trapped between the tram stop shelter and the tram itself. There wasn't much space, and things were rather chaotic. I flattened one of them with my iron bar and beat him as he was lying on the ground. A few of his buddies also ended up on the pavement. The attack lasted but a few seconds, even if those things always feel longer. We left the Nazis licking their wounds and ran.

I threw the iron bar into a ditch and my jacket into a garbage bin. The Gothenburg police did not yet know us, and there weren't as many surveillance cameras around as there are today, which is why we wore no masks. In many ways, it was an advantage not to wear masks. Without a mask, it was easy to just blend into the crowd once you'd left the scene of a crime. No one cared about a bunch of youths strolling about. Normality was our mask.

We had a quick meeting in the corner of a shopping mall, divided ourselves into pairs, and then reunited in the suburb where we were living. It was a successful action. At least one of the Nazis had to be taken to the hospital, and some others had serious injuries.

—Written by an RF founding member

THE HELIPAD

> "
>
> ***Nazi skins paraded about and beat up people who wore dreadlocks, were gay, or didn't fit their worldview for some other reason. Around Stockholm's old town, there were quarters you had to avoid if you belonged to one of the targeted groups. The Nazis usually hung out at the helipad, which had been their favorite meeting place since the 1980s.***

MEMORY "THE NAZIS AT THE HELIPAD ARE GETTING ANOTHER HIDING."

"In the early 2000s, Nazis were everywhere. They were wearing badges of their organizations and, sometimes, Nazi symbols. Not necessarily swastikas, but if you knew a little about the far right, the message was clear. You could go to the inner city on pretty much any day and be sure to encounter some of them. Their street presence was much higher than today. So when we didn't have anything else going on, we met in the inner city and went looking for Nazis to beat them up.

One summer, we gave them three beatings during one week at the very same place: the helipad in Stockholm's old town. This was their favorite hangout spot.[1] The first beating was on a Saturday, and the other two on the following Friday

The legendary helipad near the old town of Stockholm.

and Saturday. On the second Saturday, they had definitely had enough. When we exited the old town subway station that day, we ran into one of them straight away. All he said was, "Fuck, not again!" and then he ran as fast as he could, still bruised from the day before.

At the time, it was very easy to listen in on the police radio. We could hear the cops say things like, "The Nazis at the helipad are getting another hiding, send a patrol car!" That's how it was at the time. There was much more activism on the streets because the Nazis were still there and showed their convictions openly.

—Told by a former RF Stockholm member

"We Came from the Streets, We Didn't Need to Go There"

Already during the first year of RF's existence, the organization had gained a reputation beyond Gothenburg. Its structure and methods inspired others who didn't feel comfortable in the autonomous-leftist bubble. In 2003, two groups from Stockholm expressed interest independently from one another in forming a local RF chapter. Both groups consisted of SHARPs, or

RF vs. the police. Stockholm, November 30, 2004.

"Skinheads Against Racial Prejudice." They were used to beating up fascists and figured that the National Democrats were turning into an ever-bigger threat, which required a more organized response.

The national socialist National Democrats (ND) were a split from the Sweden Democrats (SD),[2] since SD had changed some of their principles: The party now accepted that people not born in Sweden could become citizens if they assimilated. For ND, this was blasphemy; they held on to what SD had always propagated: that each people had the right to retain its own culture and live as an independent nation. So while SD was preparing to enter the corridors of power, ND wanted to keep control of the streets, if necessary with the use of violence. They used events such as the Engelbrekt Day and the annual commemoration of Charles XII for a show of force,[3] and they routinely tried to silence political opponents, for example with attacks on the Pride Parade in Stockholm. In 2003, ND organized a protest against the parade, threw bottles at participants, and indiscriminately beat bystanders, including elderly people and children.

The RF Stockholm founders reckoned that ND and SD were still close ideologically, the only difference being that ND wasn't interested in the "march through the institutions." ND wanted to control the streets with force, which made them a bigger threat in everyday life.

In the following interview, founding members of RF Stockholm describe the political climate when they got in touch with RF Gothenburg:

1: There were plenty of Nazis at the time. The National Democrats seemed to be everywhere, we ran into them constantly. I have been a SHARP almost all my life. We always beat up Nazis, but we didn't understand much about politics, really. We never analyzed why Nazis were Nazis—we didn't analyze anything, to be honest, we just beat up the dickheads. I went through a period when I was a bit calmer and not even a skinhead. But when my buddy here and I met again, ND was everywhere. All those bloody marches …

When was that?
2: 2002, 2003. They were very present.

1: Yes, and even though both of us had calmed down a little, we thought, "Hey, we have no choice, we need to do something." We really weren't too keen, but ND didn't give us any options. Those fuckers had to disappear.

How violent was ND? Were they a threat?
2: They tried to establish themselves as a political party, but they did not want to lose touch with their base. They were very violent and constantly harassed people.

1: ND was like SD's stupid little brother. SD benefited hugely from sweeping their fascist roots under the rug, but ND never did that. Their members still got high on brawling in the streets. They enjoyed the violence, which was a real everyday problem. Politically, they were never as big a threat as SD, which has become very clear today. I always said that SD was the bigger threat in the long run—ND was just bunch of idiots, but we had to react. They beat up leftists, immigrants, all sorts of people on a daily basis. Their power on the streets was too big.

2: ND was founded when there was a number of relatively strong Nazi sects, also very violent. It must have been really shitty to be a member of these sects, which is why many of them turned to ND. ND provided at least an infrastructure, you got paid to do certain things, and there was a certain level of transparency. All of that attracted folks, and so they got members from NSF, Info-14,[4] and other groups—people who no longer wanted to be the lumpen of the Nazi scene, yet still brawl on occasion. ND filled a void within the political right and spoke to a whole new generation.

1: For us, violence was never a moral question. If we had to beat someone up, that's what we had to do. It was never about morality. Violence is just a tool.

What happened when you turned to RF in Gothenburg? Did they come to Stockholm for a meeting?

No, we met in Norrköping. They tried to establish a chapter there as well and wanted to hit two birds with one stone.

How was the meeting?

2: Good. Funny. They were surprised that we had gotten in touch. When we told them on the phone before the meeting that we had heard many good things about them, they said, "What?! Everyone hates us!"

1: We said, "Not us, we're like you!"

2: It was a really good meeting. We got to know each other and had a great time.

1: But it was funny too. Many of the Gothenburg folks were into football. They were GAIS or IFK supporters. For us, football wasn't a big thing, and if anyone was a supporter, then certainly not of a Gothenburg club. Yet all of the RF members who moved in hooligan circles had two things in common, regardless of whom they were supporting: They were very used to violence, and they hated Nazis. So, in that sense, it was secondary whether they supported GAIS, AIK, or Djurgården.[5]

There was of course a difference between how violence was used in RF and among the hools. RF had no rules. You could kick the shit out of people lying on the ground, jump on their heads, use weapons, attack from behind, just be all-out dirty. We didn't mess around, especially in the early years.

2: It didn't change much later either, even if some of us grew personally and became better comrades. But it is true that we were the strongest on the streets in the beginning. The comrades in Gothenburg had set the bar real high.

1: Yes, the GAIS fellas were badass.

2: A wild bunch. But we weren't too bad either, and our crew grew quickly.

What kind of people were drawn to RF?

1: It was a variety, really. But everyone was looking for a sense of unity. It felt good to be a part of RF! We were proud of it, and we were proud of what we were doing. Were we keen on beating up Nazis? Hell yeah, and no one was ashamed of that. "I kicked him in the face, and all of his front teeth were gone." "Good job, buddy! How are you feeling?!" It was always a pleasure to fuck up Nazis. But yes, it's no longer the same when you grow older, and at some point it's better when a new, hungrier generation takes over.

2: Until 2006, you could only be an RF member if you were active on the streets. We never had huge membership numbers, but we were a very tight-knit group. When this demand was dropped, it had advantages and disadvantages. The main reason for dropping it was that there were now much fewer Nazis on the streets. So we also wanted to do other things as a militant working-class organization. But if you want to expand your range of activities, you cannot expect every member to go fight Nazis on the streets. If you stick to that expectation, you will never have more than fifty members. Now, the problem was that more and more people joined RF because they liked the organization's reputation, but they themselves couldn't live up to it. They weren't tough enough.

1: I don't get off on violence as such, but I never had moral qualms about kicking a Nazi in the head. You have to leave that part of the job to those who are capable of doing it. It's not for everybody.

When you met in Norrköping, was it obvious that there were ideological differences between Gothenburg and Stockholm?

2: No, but it became clear soon. I remember that we once strolled through Gothenburg looking for Nazis but had no luck. So we talked about other things, and one of the Gothenburg people suddenly asked, "Fellas, have you heard of democratic centralism?" You should have heard our sighs! But it wasn't a big deal back then. We liked the Gothenburg folks, and we agreed to disagree. We knew that, as an organization, we'd never have ideological unity. This only became a problem later.

1: I thought it was cool that we had Trotskyists, syndicalists, and anarchists in one organization. We represented the entire far-left spectrum.

2: If you were an okay fellow who hated Nazis, you were in.

1: "Diversity in thought, unity in action," as we used to say. Our discussions were very open. I can recall proposals such as, "Why don't we kick the shit out of AFA, those sons of bitches?"

People said such things?

2: Those were exceptions. In Stockholm, RF and AFA mostly had a good relationship, we quarreled just on occasion. If RF Stockholm had been founded earlier, quite a few of the AFA members would have joined us. There were AFA members who agreed with our critique that AFA wasn't active enough on the streets. Mind you, we always knew that you don't battle fascism on the streets only. There has always been a romanticization of street fighting, even among those who can't handle it.

1: In RF, it was different. We recruited from the streets. Our members hated Nazis because they had grown up with them, fighting them for years. Now they wanted to do it in a more organized manner. That's how RF came about. We had contacts everywhere: among graffiti artists, kickers, alcoholics, ravers, drug dealers.[6] If we wanted to bash up the Nazis on football grounds, it was no problem, because we knew exactly who they were, we had our informants. We came from the streets, we didn't need to go there.

What was the relationship to the rest of the autonomous left like? It is said that you didn't care much about your reputation.

2: The autonomous left felt provoked by us, very much so. But they couldn't just ignore us. Their events, Reclaim the Streets and such, and their demonstrations were constantly attacked. They needed us for protection, and they asked for it. Then, we were there for eight hours and they left without saying goodbye. As you can imagine, we weren't exactly thrilled about that.

There were people in the autonomous left who would never have found it had it not been for RF. There is much that is attractive about the autonomous left: You can look like a fool, and it doesn't matter where you come from. But there are also many norms that you need to adapt to. RF was confusing for other leftists. We were just us, we didn't adapt to anything, and they couldn't deal with that. They felt that we were a nuisance—not necessarily each of us individually, but we as a group.

1: But that was also our strength. In RF, you didn't need to be an academic or very eloquent, and you didn't need to be a ninja or the world's best street fighter either. It was enough to be a regular kid from the suburbs. That was our pride.

"It is about time to rid our class of snakes. Put an end to the fascists!"

Was there political schooling in RF?

2: We had that discussion quite often. We ran study circles, and we moved, of course, in a political milieu. We talked a lot about politics, but there was no educational program as such. Those who were interested in political education pursued that interest mostly by themselves. We never aimed at having many members either. Essentially, we were first and foremost a self-defense organization. When people came to us with limited street-fighting experience, they became quite good at it fast, because they could trust everyone. We never left anyone behind. In other antifa groups, you couldn't be so sure about that—suddenly, everyone else was gone, you always had to watch your back. When you were with us, you had no fear.

You mean that there was a strong sense of togetherness?

2: Very strong. And there was a strong sense of loyalty, which was crucial for our success. Loyalty is always crucial when you engage in violent action, anywhere in the world. That's well documented.

Have you ever asked yourselves why there were so few women in RF?

1: What do you mean?! We were exemplary in that regard! No, seriously, I understand the question. In AFA, they discussed this a lot, equal rights for women and so on. In RF, you were a member or not, that was it. We didn't care about whether you were a man or a woman. We always said, "If you want to roll with us, you are welcome, we don't care what's under your pants."

2: We never targeted any particular groups for recruitment. New members were mostly people we had known before.

1: Man or woman, gay or straight, that didn't matter to us. All that counted was that you were ready to rumble. Yes, there was machismo, which is not surprising under these circumstances. We had no time for therapy sessions, we just followed very clear principles: either you kick that motherfucker in the face, or he will kick you. I had no patience for what qualified as "militant antifascism" elsewhere. For me, it is very simple: either you are ready to kick the shit out of that fucker or you aren't. There isn't much to talk about. When you are under attack, the only logical response is to strike back and not stop before the other one is down.

2: We got our share of criticism, of course. But self-defense is not the same as building a political movement, and the latter wasn't our primary goal, at least not in the beginning. I think the romantic image that many have of antifascism can be a problem. Antifascism is in a way the left's moral capital. And then we came along and smashed this noble image. In the eyes of many leftists, we were reckless, unpolitical, violent thugs. But there was never a discussion about what a political movement really needs. Organizations? Study circles? If we had had an agreement on this, maybe some of the conflicts we had with others on the left could have been avoided. It is perhaps an unsolved problem within the movement. For example, how diverse does a group really have to be? Of course, RF had its flaws, but I believe that much of the criticism missed its target.

Was there acknowledgment for what you did within the autonomous left?

1: Only when we kicked the shit out of the right folks.

2: Well, there was respect among some AFA members, and there were also other groups we had a good rapport with. We collaborated with No One Is Illegal, for example—they were kind of our link to the respectable left.[7] Good people. They didn't necessarily love everything we did, but their structure was similar to ours, and they had a common focus and a clear plan.

In 2006, No One Is Illegal was attacked by Nazis in Märsta, and they called you for help. Can you tell us about that?

1: The sweetest battle in history!

Okay, so the fascists had called to attack a protest by No One Is Illegal outside the detention center in Märsta, where they held people before they got deported. We took the commuter train to get there. We were highly motivated, about fifteen of us, ready to do anything. These sons of bitches had no business disrupting that protest! But it turned out that there were legions of them, and they showered the train we were on with rocks. The train was fucked, we couldn't even get out, it was a bad day for us. We had thought that we would just go there and teach them a lesson.

2: You took a few shortcuts there, but that's fine. The rocks were flying at the station in Norrviken, a couple of stops before Märsta. Unfortunately, there were people on the train who didn't trust us and desperately wanted to get out. We protected them, which meant taking plenty of rocks for them, which was no fun at all. But I'm still proud of how we handled the situation. We also managed to keep the Nazis from entering the train, and, in the end, most of them got a good hiding.

1: Yes, in the end we won, as usual.

2: But it wasn't a given that day. We were ten to fifteen, they were about thirty-five.

1: That doesn't matter, it's all a question of being organized. That day was a win, and yet it was not. I would have wanted to totally destroy those cunts.

2: Considering the circumstances, we did a good job.

1: Yes, considering the circumstances.[8]

I have heard that after that there was an RF directive to stab fascists and tell them, "This was for Märsta!" Is that true?

2: Only to some degree. It's a "truth with modifications," as we say in Sweden. But during the two weeks that followed the incident, four Nazis were stabbed and injured, that's correct.

1: But there was no directive.

2: No, it was just about sending a message.

1: There were never any directives of this kind. The level of violence was always determined by those using it.

RF felt that the autonomous left confused politics with lifestyle. Within RF, there was a lot of talk about "lifestyle politics." RF members felt that politics needed to take precedence over subculture. Most of them were skins or casuals, and the political scene was there to find comrades, not to make friends.[9]

RF members didn't look like typical left-wing activists, which also worked as a disguise during actions. On more than one occasion, fascists who were attacked by RF first thought that the RF members were fascists too. At times, people were explicitly asked to dress for actions in a way that did not make them recognizable as leftists.

RACIST MEETING PREVENTED

The following originally appeared on www.revfront.org (February 7, 2005):

The youth association of the Sweden Democrats, Sverigedemokratisk Ungdom (SDU), had planned a meeting on January 29 to found a new Stockholm chapter. The meeting was to be held in the Stockholm suburb of Alvik, but it was prevented by a joint action of AFA and RF.

SDU chairman Martin Kinnunen was welcomed in Alvik by antifascists.[10] In the course of the day, he ended up on the pavement. The antifas responsible left Alvik, but others stayed.

The frightened racists called the police, who arrived in full force. But the meeting had to be canceled nevertheless, because the remaining antifas had barricaded the building. There was some shuffling, and some more Sweden Democrats got to kiss the pavement. Eventually, too many police were around to continue hands-on education, so the antifas resorted to throwing snowballs.

The new SDU chapter could only be founded in the evening that day, at another location—probably the home

of some Sweden Democrat. Oscar Sjöstedt was elected chairman.[11] He said in a statement that SDU Stockholm was determined to pursue the path laid out on its founding day—we sure hope so!

"More Important Was That the Nazis Lost Control over the Streets Because of Us"

A particular event had a strong impact on the founders of RF Stockholm. In the early 2000s, a fifteen-year-old migrant youth accidentally walked past a White Power concert in southern Stockholm. He was beaten so badly that he ended up in a coma. The RF Stockholm founders felt that this needed a clear response. Nazis must not feel safe enough to abuse youths like that. The interviews conducted for this book make it clear that early RF members were convinced of the necessity to take the struggle against the Nazis to the streets. For them, it was the only way to stop fascism from spreading further and further.

In the following interview, one of the RF Stockholm founders tells about the ideological discussions within RF, about strategy and repression. The conversation starts with a look at the political climate in which RF Stockholm was formed:

> Nazi skins paraded about and beat up people who wore dreadlocks, were gay, or didn't fit their worldview for some other reason. Around Stockholm's old town, there were quarters you had to avoid if you belonged to one of the targeted groups. The Nazis usually hung out at the helipad, which had been their favorite meeting place since the 1980s. I wanted to do something but never felt at home at the antifascist rallies I attended. I was looking for a group where I felt safe, and since I wasn't able to find one, it seemed to make sense to found my own. I was impressed by RF Gothenburg, and so were other comrades from Stockholm. An important incident was when this fifteen-year-old Iraqi refugee was beaten into a coma after he, unknowingly, passed by a Nazi concert in

southern Stockholm. This made it clear to us that we needed to strike back. RF Gothenburg had already proven themselves to be tough motherfuckers. When Nazis get attacked, they must not be able to walk away thinking, "Oh, that wasn't too bad." No, they need to be scarred and scared, thinking about their future. The thing with this kid and the concert really was big. We often thought about him when planning actions.

What was special about RF?

RF wanted to be an organization in which politics were more important than lifestyle. Politics were always important for RF, even if, in the beginning, there was a strong focus on practical antifascism. For us, AFA did not fill this role, even if there were good AFA groups at times. When I joined RF, we weren't very close to AFA, so I don't know what they were like back then. Sorry, you asked what was special about us.

Well, neither the Nazis nor the cops had ever before met antifas who didn't look like antifas. In the early days, we could walk right into an assembly of Nazis, no problem. We were skins and hooligans, we didn't look like the leftists they knew. It was only later that some within the left copied our style—the days of the "Adidas left"! But style is one thing. More important was that the Nazis lost control over the streets because of us. That was crucial. Today, they claim that they wanted to get away from skinhead culture and that this was the reason for retreating from the streets, but that's not true, they're making that up. We chased them away, and that was a great success. We must not forget that they also tied people to them who weren't ideological Nazis, people who were simply attracted by the power they wielded on the streets. That power they lost because of us.

What goals did RF have, and how did you pursue them?

We talked about revolution, but that was very vague. Gothenburg always wanted a Leninist organization, with a central committee and such. But in practice, the ideological differences didn't matter much in the beginning. In Stockholm, we were anarchists, and the folks in Gothenburg always knew that no Leninist organization was to be made with us. But also, for them that was okay, because we had a common focus—namely, fighting Nazis. In the early days of RF, you got away with a lot. You didn't need to be too concerned about repression. I'm glad for that, otherwise quite a few of us would have disappeared behind bars quickly. We didn't think much about security, we never wore masks, even when we were at the helipad, walked through the old town, or rode the subway—all of which we did several times a week! They already had surveillance cameras back then, we just didn't care.

Can you tell us more about the street fighting? How did you build your reputation?
We were very few in Stockholm before we began to grow. At some point, we were only three people, I believe. But we all had a lot of experience in fighting. It didn't take long before everybody understood that we were raising the level of political violence to new heights. Early on, the fascists were very confused. One time, when we took new members into the city to celebrate, we ran into a bunch of Nazis. When we attacked them, one gesticulated wildly and screamed, "Hey, we are nationalists too!" They had never seen antifas who looked like us and thought we were on their side. But it didn't take long before the word got out that there was a group of skinheads who were brutal antifascists. Info-14 always taunted AFA, claiming that they were cowardly and only dared to attack when they were a hundred against one, and so on. Us, however, they described as "psychopaths on drugs." It was clear that they respected us. What did we do? We went where we could find Nazis. At the helipad, you always found some.

Did you really raise violence to new heights? Were there no other groups that did similar things?

"We speak the only language that fascists will understand."

Some AFA groups were fairly brutal too, at least during certain periods. AFA Jönköping, for example. We also collaborated with AFA Uppsala, because they would rather work with us than with AFA Stockholm. So the level of violence was perhaps not entirely new, but we maintained it like no one had done before. We were constantly looking for Nazis and attacking them. Eventually, they would practically lie down as soon as they saw us, hoping that it'd be over soon. They were scared of us.

So it was the intensity and frequency of the attacks that set you apart from other groups?

Yes, and fearlessness. Other groups often retreated when they were outnumbered. We never did. We had so much mutual trust that we felt superior even when we were outnumbered. We knew each other very well, and we knew that no one would be left behind. When we did actions with other groups, it always happened that someone was suddenly gone. Other groups even took that into account when they attacked, which is one reason why numbers were very important to them. We didn't care much about the numbers at all, we only cared about attacking with people who we knew would stand their ground. If we didn't trust someone to do that, they could not become a member.

[*The interview continues after another former RF member has joined.*]

What kind of people wanted to become members? Did that change over time?

1: We didn't care about our reputation. If people thought we were crazy, it didn't faze us. But, yes, you only attract a certain kind of people under these circumstances. Oftentimes, people with no ideology. But we weeded them out.

2: In the end, most new members were people we had known personally before.

1: In the beginning, we didn't take anyone who had ever been in AFA. We wanted to be something new, something that didn't have anything to do with the culture of AFA and the rest of the autonomous left. We had no interest in bringing in people from other leftist groups. We wanted to organize people who had never been organized. Most of our members had long had an interest in being organized, but they hadn't felt at home in AFA or similar groups. I thought it was positive that we could attract quite a lot of folks who probably wouldn't have been organized otherwise at all.

2: Ideologically, I couldn't even tell you what the difference between RF and AFA was. I just felt much more comfortable in RF.

1: AFA was a lot of dreadlocks and crusties and such.

2: People from the leftist swamp. We didn't care for them.

1: Of course, our reputation didn't help in recruiting women as members. I don't know how many times we decided in Stockholm that we would only accept new guys as members once we had recruited more women. But that took time.

2: And there never were that many.

1: It took some time before there was even one! An organization that only consists of guys is not very attractive to women. There's already a problem with sexism within the left, and within the antifascist movement it's even worse—and then you have a group allegedly consisting of nothing but dumb machos …

2: Machismo was widespread. In hindsight, we could have done things differently, especially in the beginning. It did get a little better over time. But in the early days, we were defined almost exclusively by violence and street fighting.

1: Our jargon didn't help either, we should have understood that much earlier. Our tough-guy image scared the Nazis, but it also scared others.

Which duties and responsibilities did the members have toward the organization?

1: During the first five years or so, it was very difficult to become a new member. We had to be a hundred percent sure that each new member was a person we could rely on when things got hairy. Many folks are attracted by antifascist politics without the ability to carry out antifascist action, but hardly any of them will admit that. We kept these folks away because we only accepted members who had proven themselves on the streets. If anyone had ever left a comrade's side during an action, they would have been expelled immediately.

2: That was true for the early years. Later, we also accepted members who weren't active on the streets.

1: An organization demands many qualities, not only street fighting. But one of the reasons our standards changed was that there was a lot less to be done on the streets. The Nazis were no longer there. During RF's early days, you just needed to take a stroll around town to find Nazis. Once we had chased them away, it wasn't like that. And if there are no longer opportunities for people to prove their street-fighting qualities, you have to find other criteria for membership. Protesting a Nazi gathering or attacking the home of a Nazi in the middle of the night are two very different things.

2: If we speak about duties and responsibilities, the first thing that comes to mind is that all members were expected to be active and attend meetings. Usually, we had meetings once a week, sometimes every other week. You were also expected to show up for organized activities, and some people were voted into posts—treasurer, for example.

1: You didn't need to occupy a post, but since we had a rotation system, most members eventually did. We also rotated facilitating duties at the meetings. And everyone had to give a part of their salary to the organization, I think it was 2 percent.

2: The minimum was 1 percent, I believe.

1: Maybe.

2: I was treasurer for a while. I think the minimum was one hundred crowns a month or 1 percent of your income.

1: The money was mainly used for posters and stickers. We never had any. Whatever we got, we spent.

2: I loaned RF a few thousand crowns once, and I never saw that money again.

1: Maybe, but if you robbed a Nazi of his money, you were supposed to give the money to the organization, remember that? Yet not everyone in this room did, some kept the money for themselves.

2: What?! Okay, maybe you have a point.

Back to ideology once more: How important was ideology for RF? Did your political consciousness change or develop over time?

1: We had many discussions about ideology, mostly after our meetings. But the ideological background of the members varied.

2: People who weren't political at all could not become members. In that sense, ideology did matter.

1: As far as personal development is concerned, yes, my political consciousness did develop during my time in RF. I had been active in a few groups before, but I was in RF during a big part of my adult life.

2: Same here. I found RF to be more open than other groups with respect to discussion. You could speak more freely in RF than in other leftist groups, where a different opinion or a different choice of words was often not accepted. In RF, there were no presupposed opinions, and you didn't need to be afraid of saying the wrong thing. People didn't care much about that. What counted was that we had each other's back and stuck together. If a question was controversial, we discussed it. I remember really good discussions about class struggle but also about topics such as autonomous women's organizing. Sometimes we focused on a specific topic for weeks. But that culture of discussion disappeared over time.

1: I remember facilitating a reading circle of *Under det rosa täcket* (Under the pink blanket), in which we discussed norms of masculinity and patriarchal structures.[12]

2: There were also lectures on the economy. We could have done more of that, though.

1: Yes, especially with all the members who had never been organized before. Political education should have been a bigger priority. We could have learned a lot from each other.

2: In the beginning, it wasn't easy to run meetings. People weren't used to the formalities, they spoke on top of each other, repeated themselves all the time. Once, we had a meeting just to talk about how to make the meetings better.

1: Did I call for that meeting?

2: I don't remember, but I do remember that you didn't like disorderly meetings.

1: I hate to sit in meetings where everyone speaks on top of one another. Then again, in other leftist groups it's often the same people who speak all the time.

2: I liked the rounds we did when everyone had to say something. And it wasn't enough to just say, "I agree" or "I disagree." You had to motivate your opinion. I was very young when I joined RF, and this helped me a lot. You could not just sit there in silence.

Did you face repression right from the start?

1: In the beginning, the cops didn't care about us, and not about the Nazis either. They liked neither us nor them—even though there were cops who were Nazis too. But by and large, we could do what we wanted. The cops didn't care when we got a hiding, and they didn't care when the Nazis got one. You had to be really stupid or really unlucky to get arrested. That changed, drastically, under the Reinfeldt government.[13] Suddenly, antifascism was made into a huge "danger to the public," and we had to be much more careful. Our actions needed more planning. In Gothenburg and Stockholm, the police formed special units just to observe us. In Gothenburg, there was a file with all suspected members, and when Nazis got a beating, they were allowed to go through the file in peace and quiet and identify suspects. One of us got a prison sentence for an action he wasn't even involved in, only because a Nazi had "identified" him in the file.

2: There was something similar in Stockholm under the name "Known Violent Criminals." Most of us were in it, also folks who had never been sentenced for a violent crime, so it remains a bit of a mystery as to how the cops knew that they were violent criminals. All Nazis who were beaten up were allowed to look through the file, which contained hundreds of names.

1: This had many consequences. One of us worked at a youth center. The cops called and told the board that he wasn't allowed to work there anymore. They also targeted specific individuals during demonstrations, took them to one of their vans, beat them up, and dropped them in another part of town.

2: The more notorious we became and the more actions we carried out, the harder the repression got. The sentences got harsher too, even though the brawls on the streets were fizzling out.

1: That's true. I think much of it was due to orders from above. We didn't just have the cops breathing down our neck but SÄPO too.

Now, RF had two locals, one in Gothenburg and one in Stockholm. RF Gothenburg already had bylaws and a formal structure, but with the addition of the Stockholm local, RF turned into a proper organization. The bylaws became more important, there now were common directives, and a common organizational culture developed. The locals were allowed to have their own bylaws as long as they didn't go against the general ones. Members were obliged to participate in the meetings of their respective locals. Not to attend a meeting without an acceptable excuse led to a warning. If you collected a number of warnings, you were expelled. In other words, membership in RF was more than having your name on a piece of paper. You had to be active and prioritize RF. You had to be disciplined and always strive to improve the organization and support other members. This was the approach to political work that RF members felt was missing in the rest of the autonomous left.

MEMORY "WE FINISHED OUR COFFEE AND GRABBED THE ENTIRE POLITICS SECTION. HENCE, OUR WELL-STOCKED BOOK TABLE."

"I don't know if I've already told you this story or not. Do with it what you want, but it's one of my favorite stories from that time.

We always had activities on the side. One of them was our book table. People often commented on how many books we had. The reason for it was simple, and it's a nice tale.

Some of us used to buy political literature at an antiquarian bookstore. Most of our political books came from there. The owner knew a lot about politics; he was apparently a refugee from Eastern Europe. As regular customers, we received discounts. I think he appreciated that, once a week, a group of youths showed up studying the Marxism section. The other customers were mostly middle-class ladies interested in the arts and such.

We had been frequenting the store for about two years

when, one day, the owner told us that he had to close the store. We used to chat with him and weren't happy to hear this at all. It felt like the man was a friend, and right on the spot, we promised to help him clean up the store, pack the books, and transport them to wherever he needed them to be.

Said and done. The day he had to close the store, we were there. The books he wanted to keep, we transported to his home. Without us, this would have cost him a fortune. As a gesture of gratitude, he said, "Take whatever you want for yourselves!" So we finished our coffee and grabbed the entire politics section. Hence, our well-stocked book table.

—Written by a former RF Stockholm member

"WE ARE 18.6"

> "
>
> ***There is a picture from Stockholm's Libertarian Football Cup in which we carry a banner saying "Comrades, Not Friends." That was tongue-in-cheek of course, but the point was that other leftists were comrades but not necessarily friends. That's how we felt about most other leftists, and they probably felt the same way about us. Their approach was: "Fuck, the Nazis are here, let's call RF!" But had we been invited to their event? No. As long as no Nazis showed up, we weren't welcome.***

Comrades, Not Friends

Two things tied RF members together: first, the conviction that you fought Nazis on the streets most effectively if you confronted them directly; second, the sense that you didn't fit anywhere else in the left. The latter became even more pronounced when an "RF culture" was established.

In the interviews conducted for this book, the distance that RF put between itself and the rest of the autonomous left was considered crucial for RF's identity. RF members were proud to be part of an organization that was unlike any other. AFA, too, was within the leftist milieu that RF did not want to be a part of. "Being RF" was considered special. Members spoke of "RF material" with regard to possible new recruits, and of an "RF spirit" that characterized the organization.

Below follow excerpts from interviews with three former RF members (one from Gothenburg and two from Stockholm, respectively) who joined the organization after it had been founded. They talk about why they wanted to join, and about what made RF unique.

"I Had the Impression That There Was Strong Cohesion in RF"

Why did you want to join RF?
It was more of a coincidence. I was in SUF and No One Is Illegal, so I already had experience in political organizing. When I was fifteen, I went to the demonstrations in Salem, a couple of buses went there from Gothenburg.[1] I was by myself, so I must have been pretty motivated.

At some point in 2004, I ran into an RF member. They wanted to join the "Scrap National Day" rally in Stockholm on June 6.[2] I had met RF members before, but only fleetingly, when attending assemblies as a SUF delegate or during protests.

My new RF acquaintance and I traveled to Stockholm and stayed at a friend's of his. On the way to the rally, we were ecstatic. We ran to the train station to ensure that we wouldn't be late. When we arrived downtown, we met up with more RF members and went to the helipad to beat up some Nazis. After that, the RF folks asked me if I didn't want to join. Things seemed to go well for them, and the Stockholm local had just been founded. I was ready to take the next step from SUF and focus on the topics I was most interested in.

And these topics were ...?
Antifascism and class struggle. We worked with these topics in SUF as well, but not in the way that RF did. I had the impression that there was strong cohesion in RF, that members were dedicated to the organization, and that they did good work. I was impressed by all that. It might have been a coincidence that I ran into some of them, but I liked them and I wanted to do what they did. We were a good match, we also had the same political outlook. It felt like family.

Can you specify what attracted you to RF's political work? What were the goals you associated with the organization?
I have thought a lot about what distinguished RF from other groups. I think the most important aspect was that the founders did not have a long history in political organizing. The norms and conventions of the left didn't matter to them. That was unique. Sure, the organization was very male-dominated, and things could get rough. But the goals were clear: fight fascism and class society! There were ambitions to do more community and union work, but in the end, antifascism always came first. In hindsight, this wasn't ideal perhaps. It would have been interesting to see how far we could have come had we given more attention to other things.

When you became a member, was it still expected to be active on the streets?
Yes, that was still expected.

Why did that change?
It took some time. I'm not even sure if the bylaws required street activism, or if it was simply assumed that that's what everyone was going to focus on. It took six to seven years before it was okay for members to focus on other things.

You said that RF felt like family when you joined. Did that remain so?
RF changed over time, of course. There were ups and downs. In the beginning, the sense of family was very strong, but dynamics changed once there were more locals. Everything became more structured, which was inevitable. But there was always a strong sense of togetherness.

RF essentially started out as a circle of friends and turned into a nationwide organization. Would you say that RF was organized horizontally?
The most important decisions were all made at the nationwide

meetings, where each voice was heard. I liked those meetings. Gothenburg and Linköping often agreed with one another, and so did Stockholm and Örebro. Stockholm and Örebro were more anarchist, Gothenburg and Linköping more communist, to put it simply.

The nationwide meetings determined the direction of the organization. We discussed the internal dynamics, and many other things. The locals had to adapt to the conditions of their respective cities and regions. But we were not like AFA, where the locals were completely autonomous. In my opinion, the problem with completely autonomous is that there are always informal leaders. I thought it was good that we had the nationwide meetings to make common decisions. Sure, even on a nationwide level, there were people who were more influential than others, that's always the case. But within RF, this was never destructive—everyone could raise their voice.

When you were an RF member, the far-right group Gothenburg's Free Nationalists (GFN)*[3] *wielded power on the streets. Was fighting them a priority for you?

Of course, that was very important! Just like us, GFN focused on street activism. We were constantly brawling. There were periods when we met every day at 8 or 9 a.m. to go look for GFN. Show me kids today with that discipline! We weren't very schooled politically, but we were disciplined, and we organized ourselves, creating a base for long-term political work. We were very young, but we formed an organization that attracted people from the working class, people who had never been politically active before. We can be proud of that, and no one can take that away from RF.

There was a lot of violence. Did that impact you personally?

Of course you are impacted by that. Violence becomes normalized, and reservations about using it gradually disappear. But I think that our violence was directed toward violent people and organizations. It's important to keep that in mind.

Do you still stand behind what RF did?
I think that, as an organization, RF did great work when considering our political convictions and the social context we found ourselves in. RF motivated people to get involved in antifascist and socialist politics who otherwise might have never gotten involved in political work. That was a success.

As far as our methods go, that's difficult to evaluate. A conviction is right or wrong, it doesn't have to be measured against empirical outcome. With methods, it's different. Our methods did have a clear outcome: Many left the fascist movement because of us, and the fascists disappeared from the streets. But these are complex questions, and many things need to be considered.

My political convictions remain the same, but how to best reach your goals always needs to be reconsidered. I think it would have been very interesting to see what we could have achieved politically had the focus on antifascism not been so strong. Then again, in an organization such as RF it might have been difficult to focus on anything else. Labor unions operate under different conditions than RF did. But I am proud of what we have done, and I feel a strong connection to RF and all its members to this day.

How was it to be in prison as an RF member?
Prison is prison, but considering the circumstances it was good. I almost felt guilty because I received so much mail. Where I was, all inmates picked up the mail together after lunch, so everyone could see what the others received. Some never received any mail, not a single letter, and it couldn't have felt nice to see me receive so much. I am very grateful for all the support!

How did your prison term affect your political activism?
Not in any significant way. But it did affect people who were close to me, especially my family. I wanted to avoid another prison term under all circumstances. Many of us

> approached the matter thus: One term was okay, that was part of the activism we had chosen, and we accepted that. It was almost impossible to avoid. But another term? No thanks. Then, you really feel the consequences, it's hard to get a job, and so on.

In the interviews conducted for this book, former RF members reflected a lot on how their political activism affected them personally. A section dedicated to the (negative and positive) consequences of using violence for political ends follows further below.

"Hey, Are You Nationalists Too?"

In the following interview, a former RF Stockholm member reflects on the RF slogan "Comrades, Not Friends":

> *Describe the political climate on the streets when you joined RF!*
> It was not like today. Nazis were everywhere, and they wore their White Power shirts openly. Antifascist resistance on the streets was necessary in a way it isn't today. Leftist events were constantly threatened.
>
> *Why did you join RF and not AFA?*
> I didn't even know what the exact difference was, but I felt that RF was a better fit for me. I had some insight into AFA, and there was a lot of political correctness, it was more your typical activist culture. RF members came from the suburbs, they were like my childhood friends but political. They talked differently.
>
> *How did you become a member?*
> I met RF members at political events, and eventually I was invited to have a chat with them about possibly joining. The rules for how to become a member changed constantly.
>
> *You joined in 2004. Were there even rules at the time?*

There were rules, but they weren't strictly enforced. Most new members were friends of folks who were already members. In the beginning, we were a small circle, it was easy to keep track. We only needed more formal rules when people applied for membership who we didn't know.

During its first years, RF was mainly active on the streets. There was a lot of violence. Did that attract you?
You have to put all of that into perspective. Yes, we beat up Nazis, but that was necessary at the time. I think we figured it needed to be done to make political activism possible. Today, the Nazis no longer control the streets, so our reasoning might seem difficult to understand. But back then, they were a serious problem.

It seemed important for RF to disassociate itself from the autonomous left, is that right?
With respect to AFA, it was complicated. Sometimes the relationship was good, and sometimes it wasn't. There were always good people in AFA, but members changed frequently. Members in RF stayed much longer. In general, we didn't have a very good relationship with the autonomous left.

How did that affect you as an organization?
I thought it was a good thing. Other members had different views, but I always felt we should do our own thing, and I think that was what the majority felt. It was bothersome to work with others, much easier to decide for yourself and get to work. Maybe we were a little peculiar, but I thought that's how it should be.

But you were part of Network Against Racism,[4] *for example ...*
Network Against Racism was a good initiative, but in general I never thought that RF should join broader alliances. There were certain things that we were good at, and I felt we should focus on them. I wasn't against cooperation, as long

"Comrades, Not Friends." Stockholm's Libertarian Football Cup, ca. 2008.

as cooperation meant that we contributed with what we were good at, not with what others wanted us to contribute with. There is a picture from Stockholm's Libertarian Football Cup in which we carry a banner saying "Comrades, Not Friends."[5] That was tongue-in-cheek of course, but the point was that other leftists were comrades but not necessarily friends. That's how we felt about most other leftists, and they probably felt the same way about us. Their approach was: "Fuck, the Nazis are here, let's call RF!" But had we been invited to their event? No. As long as no Nazis showed up, we weren't welcome.

Was it a conscious choice to be "peculiar" and "do your own thing"?

Yes, I would say so, but it also just happened, in a way. The people drawn to RF were not the kind of people you would find in the autonomous left otherwise. We came from the suburbs, we had a different background, violence was familiar to us. Yes, there was machismo, but that came with the terrain.

RF was often criticized for that. Do you think the critique was justified?
I'm sure it often was. We did many good things, but we also made mistakes—the macho stuff, the flirts with hooliganism, those things weren't good, and we should have made a bigger effort to correct them. But it wasn't easy amid all the violence.

What was RF's strategy, both for activism on the streets and political work more broadly?
Strategies developed over time. We looked normal and didn't want to look like the rest of the left. The Nazis often thought we belonged to them. It was a classic to start an attack by approaching them with the question "Hey, are you nationalists too?" Then we started swinging the second they emphatically said, "Yes!" I'm not sure if that's a strategy, but we never wanted to be like the rest of the left. Whenever we got the feeling that we were becoming too much like them, we said, "Wait a minute! Everyone else is doing this, so why should we do it? We must figure out something else!"

Do you remember all members being forced to fight on the streets?
You were never forced to do anything. What was expected was that you were active. If you missed a few meetings without a proper excuse, you were expelled. One thing was always clear: If you wanted to be an RF member, you had to show commitment, you couldn't just sit at home. Sure, things can happen in your personal life, but you had to be engaged. And in the early years, we only had members who wanted to fight. That some wanted to do other things only became an issue later. Most important was to be honest with yourself. When you said that you were ready to join an action, you couldn't just run away, but it was okay if you said that you weren't up for it.

What happened when someone made a mistake?
There were no clear rules. When we realized that members had very limited political knowledge, we encouraged them to

educate themselves. Our starting point was to help members who had troubles with certain aspects of our work, not to exclude them. What's the point of excluding people just because they don't do something in the exact way that others expect from them? There were margins for error in RF, which I'm sure had its disadvantages as well, but overall I thought it was good. Many of our members wouldn't have found a place in other leftist organizations because of the way they talked. But where I come from, you call people a "cunt," and yes, you can question that, but do you need to exclude or silence people because of it? Shouldn't you talk to them instead? We were never your usual leftist organization. When we ran into problems, we resolved them in ways that fit the organization.

Did you talk much about class politics in RF?
Absolutely. Let's put it this way: Until 2004, we mainly did antifascist work, we were constantly on the streets, the Nazis were there, we were young, we wanted to see action. But then other political work became more and more important, and class struggle was the foundation of our politics. We always emphasized that.

How important was political ideology for you?
It was important, but we had differences within the organization, not least between Gothenburg and Stockholm. In Gothenburg, folks were communists, in Stockholm anarchists.

Do you remember that creating problems?
Sometimes we disagreed on things, but it didn't create big problems.

Did you ever question violence as a political means?
There was a bit of back and forth. In the beginning, before I joined, the message was clear: "We are active on the streets, we beat up Nazis, that's it." But then there was a turn toward class struggle.

"Workers' power? Democracy? Alienation? This is about class!"

And that meant less violence?
We chose the means that we considered best. Our class politics didn't rely on violence, but our reputation came in handy.

Did you have formal leaders?
No. We tried to make decisions by consensus. There are always people who are particularly active and who have more sway than others, but everyone had a say. At least that's how it was in Stockholm. We had facilitators at our meetings, but the task rotated and everyone had to do it, even if we weren't all equally good at it. I thought that was positive. It was impossible for people to just sit there and think, "All right, someone else is saying the same thing I would have said, so I don't have to say anything." We also divided responsibilities on the streets as much as possible.

Did you decide before each action who would be in charge of it?
A street action is not the same as a members' meeting. If someone makes an error during a street fight, it can have

serious consequences. We used certain criteria, such as: "You know this neighborhood, you know what can be done here, you're in charge!"

So someone was in charge of the action?
Yes.

How did RF change during the years you were a member? Were the changes positive or negative?
We became more mature, which, I believe, also made the organization better. When I left RF in 2009, I think some errors had been made and the organization had lost its soul. New people entered, and RF became more like other leftist groups. But that was a subjective impression, maybe it wasn't true. While I was still a member, we started transitioning from street fighting to broader class politics. I thought that was needed.

The fascists disappeared from the streets. How did that affect morale in RF? Did you maintain the same level of activity?
Antifascist work attracts people. Class politics less so, which makes the question of how to do it right a difficult one. When Nazis threaten leftist events, your goal is clear: You have to protect the events and keep the Nazis at bay. It is clear who the bad guys are, and it is pretty clear what you gotta do: Nazis don't like to get beaten up, so you beat them up and try to make them disappear. With class politics, it gets more complicated. But the focus on class politics was right and necessary.

When you left RF, was it still important for the organization to distance itself from other leftist groups?
Not in the same way as before, I believe, but I'm not sure. The many new members did, of course, change the organization. I felt that some of them were more at ease with the autonomous left than we, the earlier members, were, but maybe

I'm wrong. You could never be an RF member without any political consciousness, but in the beginning we were real outsiders within the left. The distance to other groups was huge. The stronger we became as an organization, the easier it probably became to collaborate with us. We became relatively popular, and many people wanted to join.

In hindsight, what would you say about RF's propaganda? I'm mainly thinking of the videos you uploaded. What did they mean to you?
The videos were great propaganda. At the same time, they confirmed the image of RF as a macho organization. I think the propaganda was positive for the most part, even if there are always negatives.

Could this work in the same way today?
Today, the political climate is different. Back then, you ran into Nazis every time you went downtown, especially on the weekends. Today, you can prowl the inner city for an entire year without seeing a Nazi. So, back then, there was a reason for what we did. The left had no respect on the streets, they were ridiculed by the Nazis: "Yes, they might make a move when it's ten against one …" We changed that. In Gothenburg, fights with Nazis were often introduced with the line "Have you heard of RF?" That became notorious. Eventually, it was enough to utter those words for the Nazis to basically lie down and surrender. They became tired of running into us and retreated from the streets. Before we were there, they could do whatever they wanted. A couple of years later, they didn't even dare to distribute flyers. They knew that we would find them and fuck them up.

People say that you never lost a fight. How is that possible?
In the beginning, all our members were experienced street fighters. We had each other's back, we never left anyone behind. The trust we had for each other was enormous.

"Even if They Were Ten and We Were Two, We Had to Teach Them a Lesson"

In the following interview, a former RF Stockholm member talks about how he had never thought about joining a political organization before discovering RF:

What was the political climate like when you joined RF?
The far-right scene was changing. Many of them were still on the streets and you saw their symbols, but they began ... well, they wanted to get away from the skinhead thing. There were more of these—what shall we call them?—hooligan Nazis.

In the suburbs or in the inner city?
Both, I would say. We still had Nazis in the suburbs who looked the way you'd imagine a stereotypical Nazi to look like. In the inner city, it was a little different. But then the Nazi hools also spread to the suburbs.

How did you get in contact with RF?
I had plenty of fights with Nazis in secondary school. The Nazis were our age, maybe a little older, and some had older siblings. But they weren't a great problem before they got in touch with Nazis from the neighboring suburbs. Then, there were so many that we sometimes had to run. I hated that, so we tried to get in touch with AFA through the friend of a friend. We wanted AFA to help us keep those Nazis in check. We had a meeting with them at Kafé 44, but my sense was that they didn't take us seriously.[6] They sat there and acted cool, but they didn't want to promise anything, even though I could provide them with information about the day and time the Nazis would gather next. Well, by complete coincidence, I met folks from the Little League shortly thereafter.[7] I don't even know if they were already RF members at the time or still hangarounds, but regardless, they promised to help us. And they did. They came that day I thought the Nazis would meet. There were only four of them, fewer than what we

had expected, but we figured we'd have to make the best of it. However, when we went to the Nazis' usual meeting place, they weren't there! Anticlimax. We stayed in contact nonetheless, because we figured they might be able to help us again, and we did meet thereafter, also with other folks who had just become RF members.

You never considered joining a different political group?
No. RF were my people! They shared my background, we had things in common. No spectacular explanation, but that's how it was. I had never thought much about joining any organization. I was eighteen, I liked militant antifascism, and I attended demonstrations, but getting organized seemed to be for others. AFA was too subcultural for me. In RF, I felt at home, and we fulfilled an important task. In a sense, I continued what I had started in secondary school, just on a bigger scale.

Did your political consciousness develop while you were in RF?
Yes and no. Many of my childhood friends were Chileans—Latin Americans in general, but mainly Chileans. I was drilled politically from an early age.[8] There was a lot of talk about politics, and I considered joining the Young Left. But I soon realized that this wasn't for me. RF deepened my political consciousness, but there had already been a foundation. With time, RF moved away from pure antifascism. Or let's say we paid more attention to fascism as a result of capitalism.

Was there a strategy for your antifascist work?
Yes, and it was simple and clear: We went to where the Nazis were and were determined not to allow them to feel safe ever. We wanted them to get scared and fuck off. This could only be done through violence, there was no other way. Nazis on the streets aren't just an eyesore, they are a threat to many people. You can only get rid of that threat through violence.

Can you recall discussions where violence as a political means was questioned?

We discussed violence a lot. Was it right to use violence under all circumstances? Were there times when it shouldn't be used? But we rarely came to that conclusion. In hindsight, maybe we should have been more restrained at times. The repression might not have gotten so hard. In that sense, the violence was perhaps counterproductive. But our goal was to rid the streets of Nazis, and for that, violence was a necessary evil.

Once the Nazis had retreated from the streets, did you consider other means?

In the early years of RF, we followed a simple code: "Whenever, wherever, and in whatever way." The Nazis were not allowed to ever feel safe. Even if they were ten and we were two, we had to teach them a lesson. We attacked anyway, using whatever means we had available. It worked. The Nazis got scared and avoided entire areas. They ran, even when we were outnumbered. We chased them into a kind of shadow world.

Then there was a phase when they were better prepared. During that phase, the fights turned into hooligan-type fights, but with weapons. Maybe we should have turned to home visits already then, more classical antifa style: ten against one outside of their homes, being a pest in everyday life.[9] But we stuck to the street battles. We had thought we had won the streets, but maybe you never win as long as Nazis are still around, wherever they might hide.

How did you see the relationship between RF and the rest of the autonomous left?

We had a decent relationship with some groups, especially AFA, but there were always RF members who felt we shouldn't have relationships with any other group. Me and others didn't think that way, and then there were those who

didn't care. In any case, the relationships we had were all on a personal level. We had no official relationships with other groups, especially not in the beginning. In Stockholm, AFA benefited from RF appearing on the scene. We made antifascism popular, and that got them new members too—even if those people should have come to us!

So the relationship to AFA Stockholm was okay?
On a personal level, it always was, but from about 2007, we also collaborated officially.

There's a banner from 2006 that carries the name of both groups.
Yes, that was from National Day protests that year. It was kind of the signal for official collaboration. But even before that, we sometimes coordinated actions and exchanged information. Together we chased the AIK Nazis who disrupted Pride.[10] Neither we nor AFA could have done it alone. A difference always was that all of our members were active on the streets, which wasn't the case with AFA. They had some members doing other things. We only had that later on.

When did you realize that your actions brought results and that the number of fascists on the streets went down?
Quite early on, really, but I'm not sure if the Nazis understood that we were the reason. They always spoke of a "small, militant group" they had to watch out for. Later, they understood who that group was. We had access to their internal communication, and they wrote things like, "AFA is not a problem as long as there aren't too many of them—but these folks from RF, with their work pants and knives, they are completely nuts." They were nervous, which was good for us. I noticed it in my suburb too. When it became known that I was in RF, I only had to show up somewhere for the Nazis to run. It wasn't anything about me personally, just the group I belonged to and its reputation.

What was the relationship like with the other RF locals?
It was very good! One reason might have been that RF locals hardly had relationships with any other groups. Sometimes the reason was open conflict, sometimes it was just petty stuff. Most RF locals were quite isolated.

When you left in 2009, was there still the same sense of togetherness and mutual trust as in the beginning?
Yes, at least among the seasoned members. But the organization was changing. In 2009, we had members who would say things like, "If I have to, I'll come along for the action, but I'd rather not." You can never fully trust people who you don't do actions with. But there were still people in the group who I trusted 110 percent.

Was RF organized horizontally?
Some people always have more influence than others. That's natural and related to personality, charisma, and leadership qualities. There are some who like to speak and some who don't. But in general RF was organized horizontally.

How important was political ideology?

We spoke a lot about ideology and tried to initiate reading circles. But there are two responses to that question. The first one is that you were welcome in RF as long as you weren't a misogynist, a right-wing fool, or some petty liberal. You needed to hate Nazis and be willing to punch them. The second response is that political organizing means more than just showing up for meetings. You need an ideology to stand on, you need to understand where fascism comes from. You don't need to have read *Capital* or have some fancy theory about the current significance of Bakunin—well, some might think you do, but I don't. What you must have is an understanding of current social developments. You need to know who's responsible for waging wars, and which political questions the right is exploiting for their interests. These things are important. What Marx said on page 704 of *Capital* is not.

I have heard that people applying for membership in RF Gothenburg had to write a short text explaining their politics. Was there anything similar in Stockholm?
Oh, they had that in Gothenburg? No, we didn't have anything like that, or at least I can't remember it. But when there suddenly were people who wanted to become members without anyone knowing them, we had to change our routines. We did interviews and such.

Were the ideological differences within the organization obvious?
Yes. But in Stockholm, we didn't care much. You could hear things like, "You only say that because you are an anarchist," or, "That's just because you are a bloody authoritarian communist," but it didn't really have any impact on our work. But in Stockholm, unlike in Gothenburg, the anarchists were the majority. Whenever we had nationwide meetings, the differences were quite pronounced. We had many discussions about whether we should take the organization into a more libertarian or a more authoritarian direction.

Do you recall the discussions about the central committee?
I remember discussions from 2008. I was totally opposed, but I can't really remember much about the discussions themselves.

RF distanced itself from the rest of the autonomous left. When leftist groups formed alliances, for example to protest Nazi marches, RF carried out its own actions. Many former members say that they didn't care about the broader left at all and focused fully on building their own structures. They didn't want to be part of the "left middle class," which they felt dominated other leftist groups. RF was original, not a copy of other organizations. Members were proud of their working-class roots and RF culture.

MEMORY "WHEN IT'S TIME TO BAIL, THE NAZI LIES THERE COVERED IN CUTLERY, BROKEN PLATES, A CHAIR, AND A GIGANTIC SHIP'S WHEEL."

"One of the biggest and craziest actions I was part of started at the Gothenburg district court. It must have been in 2004. A bunch of Nazis who had abused and injured left-wing youths were put on trial. The courthouse was in a small alley in the inner city of Gothenburg. We were a big group who showed up: members from RF and AFA, antifascist football fans, and other activists and friends. All in all, we were a little more than fifty people. This is how I recall the day …

We are standing in a yard close to the entrance to the courthouse. When the Nazis come out, accompanied by a few cops, four or five of us jump into the alley and cut off the Nazis' way. The cops—maybe eight of them, no riot gear—form a line to protect the Nazis. The Nazis think they are safe and start taunting our comrades with slogans and laughter. They don't understand that there are plenty more of us hiding nearby.

Eventually, our comrades in the alley give us the sign to join them. Now the fun starts. We charge out of the yard in masks, all carrying projectiles we took from a nearby coffee shop: glass bottles, cups, and glasses. The cops are caught by total surprise and attempt to shield the Nazis. Some bottles and cups fly over their heads, and some of the Nazis try to escape into a side alley. We can't let them get away, and when some of us yell, "Let's go!" we storm the police line, linking arms. What happens next, none of us could have anticipated: The cops flee into the courthouse and barricade the door. Some Nazis manage to follow them inside, but most of them are running toward the harbor.

Before reaching the harbor, they have to cross a busy, multilane road with cars doing fifty miles an hour. We hear tires squealing and cars skidding while we're chasing them. At the harbor, the Nazis split into several small groups, trying to get away in different directions. Some of them end up on a boat that serves as a restaurant. A few comrades and I follow. We shortly lose sight of them, but then we see them on the upper deck and race up the stairs. They run into the kitchen, but I manage to cut off the way for one of them. Now he's all alone in the dining room with his NSF hat on. I almost burst out laughing when telling him that it's a bad day for a hat like that.

He grabs a chair to protect himself. I grab another chair and pin him against the wall. At that moment, a few less experienced antifascists arrive. They have brought glasses, plates, and cutlery, which they all throw at him. It allows me to get to him from the side and pin him to the floor; now he is caught between the chair's legs and unable to move. The other antifascists keep throwing stuff at him, and some are kicking him. I hold on to the chair that renders him helpless. Eventually, one antifascist tears a huge, old wooden ship's wheel from the wall and throws it at him. When it's time to bail, the Nazi lies there covered in cutlery, broken plates, a chair, and a gigantic ship's wheel.

We leave the boat and meet the comrades who have beaten up the Nazis in the kitchen. None of the Nazis got

> away that day; they all got their beatings, even the ones who made it to the nearby opera house.
>
> —*Written by a former RF Gothenburg member*

Youngest but Fiercest

Officially, you had to be eighteen years old to become an RF member, but the age limit was never strictly enforced, at least not during the early years of the organization. In Stockholm, people turned a blind eye when they met four youths who had lured NSF members into a trap by offering gas masks to sell online. Of course, the youths had no intentions to sell gas masks but instead planned to jump them.

One of these youths, who would soon form the unofficial youth wing of RF Stockholm, remembers the following about their first meeting with RF members:

> We often hung out downtown trying to find and beat up Nazis. We had tried to join AFA, but they hadn't taken us because we were too young. Then one day we ran into RF members and told them that we were on our way to meet folks from NSF. The RF members asked whether they could come along, but we said, "No, this is our thing!" So we went to meet the fashes and kicked the shit out of them, and the RF members were very impressed. We were only fourteen years old, the Nazis were significantly older. I was quite frail and always sprained my wrists fighting. Anyway, that's how we became part of RF, and they called us the Little League, since we were so young.

The Little League inspired more youths to join RF. Once, there was a brawl in downtown Stockholm between fascists and the Little League, who had brought along a group of young SHARPs. These SHARPs went on to form the group Antifascist Skinheads (AFS), which also became part of the wider RF circle. One of them remembers first meeting the Little League:

> It was in 2004 or 2005 when I got to know the Little League. My friends and I had many problems with Nazis in our suburbs. By accident, we met the Little League downtown. We drank together and fought Nazis, and for the first time I felt that there was real antifascist resistance, that is, other people who saw the same problems as us and were ready to strike back. Most of the folks I knew simply started running when they saw fascists.

ASF would soon be part of a new layer that was added to RF: people who did not want to be members but who were willing to join actions. RF members had brought friends to actions before, and also to meetings. This was now formalized under the name Operative Units (OU). Officially, the OU system was introduced in 2007. It made much bigger RF actions possible.

How the Little League members managed to join RF despite their tender age is explained by two former RF members:

> **1:** The Little League. What a bunch of crazy motherfuckers! They were notorious for stabbing fascists without blinking. We were used to beating them, and we had cut some fascists with knives before, but the Little League took this a step further: "We don't fuck around, we stab them!" Street violence 2.0, they cannot deny that. They stabbed and asked questions later.
>
> **2:** Yes, we took them in, but we wouldn't have done it had they not wanted to join. However, I'm not sure whether it was the right thing to do. I've thought about it a lot. We exposed them to a lot of violence and drugs. At the time, we thought that was okay, even though they were only fourteen. We figured that this would be a part of their life soon anyway, so it was only good that we could keep an eye on them. Well, today, one of them is dead, and two others became criminals—luckily, they rounded the corner and are great people now. Anyway, when we speak of the Little League, we're probably speaking of the

> most dangerous antifascists Sweden ever knew. But I am no longer twenty and would probably no longer take them in. Essentially, we threw them into cold water with a keg of beer and a pouch of drugs and said, "Swim!"

The Little League and the youths who joined RF alongside them were probably also the youngest organized antifascists that Sweden ever had.

AFA had a stricter age limit than RF. They didn't accept members who hadn't been politically schooled either. But they had the AFA Youth for some time, in which people under the age of eighteen could get organized. Former RF members believe that this was in response to the Little League.

RF Gothenburg wasn't very strict with the age limit either. They recruited on the streets, and political schooling was not a strong criterion for membership. But RF placed a bigger emphasis on political education than AFA did. We will return to this.

MEMORY "WHEN I TURN AROUND, I SEE A CUTE LITTLE CAT WITH A LOPSIDED FACE POUNDING ON A NAZI."

"I was cruising in a Stockholm suburb with another RF member when we saw an active Nazi by the name of Niklas "Warzone." He was mainly active online. "Warzone" was his moniker.

So we see him stroll by, and my comrade says that he needs a mask to attack him, because Warzone might recognize him otherwise. I follow Warzone while my comrade runs into a shopping center to get a mask. Warzone heads for a bus stop and waits. I see that his bus will arrive in three minutes and text my comrade to hurry up if he wants to be part of this. He answers that he is on his way and should make it in time. He does, and the two of us follow Warzone onto the bus.

When Warzone gets off, so do we. Warzone follows a bicycle path, and we catch up with him and say, "Excuse me!" He turns around and, *boom*, we land our first punch. The two of us are pounding on Warzone and say, "You are Niklas Warzone, you might try to hide online, but we'll find you!" Everything goes very quickly. The entire attack takes maybe fifteen seconds. Warzone is on the ground and doesn't resist.

Only now do I look at my comrade, who has obviously gone into a toy store to get a mask—a white cat mask, to be exact, and being in a hurry he clearly didn't pay attention to the size, because he got one for eight-year-olds, which is way too small for him and only covers half his face. The holes for the eyes sit way too close together, which is why he has put on the mask diagonally, to at least see from one eye. While I walk away from Warzone, my companion gets another few kicks in, and when I turn around, I see a cute little cat with a lopsided face pounding on a Nazi.

By the way, Niklas stopped being a Nazi after that, at least an active one.

—Told by a former member of RF Stockholm/Little League

"Whenever, Wherever, and in Whatever Way"

All former RF members who were interviewed for this book confirm the strong Nazi street presence common when RF was founded. They say that a visit to the inner cities of Gothenburg, Örebro, or Stockholm inevitably led to encounters with Nazis, especially on the weekends. Fascists were always around. Either they were known figures from the Nazi scene or people who wore their ideology on their sleeves. The antifascists' strategy was simple: They went to the places where the Nazis gathered and attacked them. The goal was to instill fear in them and reclaim the streets.

RF members were familiar with violence. Many had a long history of fighting fascists. They had no doubt about what to do when they encountered a Nazi, no matter whether they were alone or with comrades. "Whenever, wherever, and in whatever

"Struggle without compromise—in school, at work, on the streets."

way" was the code they followed, meaning that when, where, and how a fascist was attacked didn't matter; it could be during rush hour traffic in the subway or near a surveillance camera. This was in the early 2000s; repression against antifascists only became a serious problem in later years.

With RF never pulling back when they saw a chance to attack and none of their members ever getting badly injured, they became notorious in Nazi circles. They turned attacks in which they were outnumbered into an advantage, as it increased their "violent capital."[11]

One of the fascist groups that RF Stockholm was facing during the early years was the Anti-Red Front, which, in RF lingo, was called the "McDonald's gang." It was a group of fascists who, in 2005, gathered in the inner city, especially at the McDonald's restaurant on Sergels Torg.[12] They threatened and attacked people and posed a danger to many folks. It was easy for RF to confront them, since they always met at the same place. There were regular fistfights between the groups, which helped RF Stockholm build strength and confidence. Former RF Stockholm members say that these fights really tied them together as a group. In Gothenburg, the fights with GFN had a similar function, leading to the notorious opening line "Have you heard of RF?" turning into a force of its own. RF had built itself a reputation.

2005-2009

"OUR MERE EXISTENCE POSED A THREAT TO THEM"

"

In order to understand where we find ourselves today, and why we are gathered here, we need to know our history and our background. The basic ideas and values of RF were created during this history. We are proud of it, and everybody here shall know about it. RF was founded by five people who were tired of being ostracized by the autonomous left. We had the burning desire to change the world, but the left's so-called activism frustrated us—to the point where working in any of the existing leftist groups no longer was an option.

Even though critiquing the autonomous left was important for RF's identity, the organization repeatedly showed willingness to engage in dialogue and, on occasion, also to collaborate with other groups on the left. We will look at minutes from a nationwide meeting in 2006 further below. Before that, however, we will hear two former members speak about the "RF spirit," the "macho left," and the significance of Red Action for RF.[1]

"Fuck Them and Their Mothers!" or "While the Rest of the Left Fought Among Themselves, We Fought the Right"

Was the critique that RF was macho justified?
1: Haha, yes, the "macho left" was a big thing. Yelah published an article titled "Macho Leftists Are Not Our Friends." *ETC* even ran the headline "RF—Not Our Comrades!"[2]

2: *ETC* weren't really our comrades, and the folks at Yelah weren't either. Fuck them and their mothers!

1: I think the term "macho left" was justified in some ways, even if I don't see myself as macho. Here is the thing: RF's main issue was class, nothing else mattered to us. Or, other things did matter, but class was central. Class incorporates gender rights and all those questions, but it's true, we didn't pay much attention to them. I remember when SD came to Nyköping during their election campaign, and one of our Black members yelled, "All right, come here, you pussy-ass faggots!" The result of such incidents was always the same. In this case, no one talked about us traveling to fucking Nyköping to stop SD, all they wanted to talk about were the inappropriate words some of us were using. Sure, the wording wasn't state of the art, but to be honest, I didn't care much about these things. For others, however, it confirmed what they thought they already knew: We were machos who read Marx, got off on violence, and fucked up Nazis. Well, I understand that it might have looked like that from the outside.

2: Well, the image wasn't entirely false, but RF's big strength was to organize people with socialist values who hated Nazis and class society, but …

1: … didn't fit in with the left.

2: Exactly! And in that context, you might hear words you don't like. But in comparison to the fucked-up rest of the Swedish left, we had actual working-class people in our ranks, and where we come from, people talk like that. It's not great, and people should kick the habit, but no one should be excluded because of it. While the rest of the left fought among themselves, we fought the right.

1: Eventually, we used the term "macho left" for ourselves.

2: Yes, it became an identity.

1: When people throw shit at you, you will eventually claim that shit. Once, when I was responsible for our May 1 rally, the slogan was "We remember Amalthea—100 years

"1908–2008: We remember Amalthea—100 years of class hatred!" Stockholm, May 1, 2008.

of class hatred!"[3] I wanted our route to cross that of the anarchists, because their march was always so shitty. But someone called me the night before, insulting me: I was a chauvinist male RF pig, and so on. They even threatened me: They'd pay me a visit and "settle the score" and whatnot. I simply invited them to our May 1 party. Nobody showed up, but they loved to hurl insults at us: "You are the leftist equivalent to NMR!"[4] At some point, you identify with accusations like that, kinda like: "Okay, you think that's what we are? Fine, we'll be that way."

One hundred years after Amalthea? So that must have been in 2008. How was it in 2014, shortly before RF dissolved? Did people still have the same image of the organization?

2: I think it got a little better. After all, we were still here but our fiercest critics weren't. I suppose they had gotten comfortable in their middle-class lives or returned to their fucking universities. I don't know, in any case they were gone. The new generation of activists had more understanding for us. Plus, we were no longer as raw as in the beginning.

1: Yes, we had grown older. But back to the term "macho left": I think it's a fucked-up term. I don't see myself as macho, but I identified with the term for some time because people were constantly using it against me. Okay, maybe we ran our mouths, maybe we liked to fight, but when you have this label hanging over you, it is not good for your political development, and it wasn't good for our political work. I stand by it: We were no machos.

2: I think it depends on what you mean by that.

1: Okay, here is what I think: If you call a girl "fat" all the time when she's little, she'll probably have body issues growing up. If you call someone an "idiot" all the time, they will eventually think they're an idiot. At some point, this will become a part of their identity. And when those you think you're defending hate you, you will also eventually feel like an idiot. We had women in our organization—were they also part of the macho left?

2: I think those who used that term for us have never experienced real macho culture. They have never sat in a room full of construction workers or in prison. They probably don't come from the suburbs either. They don't know that world. And since we didn't fit into their world, we were macho, that's how I see it. And so we claimed that name.

1: Look at the Yelah article: I think we were only mentioned by name once, but it was clear that the article was about us. Not AFA, not SUF, not the SAC.[5] We were the great threat for the feminist movement. I really didn't get that.

What kind of people were drawn to RF?

2: We were looking for people with certain values—values that you find among certain people. It could be norm-breaking women or queers, but also regular kids from the suburbs. It was all about honor, loyalty, and violence—that's what we were looking for, because that's what we needed.

1: In the Operative Units, we needed people who wouldn't run when the shit hit the fan. That was the entire purpose of the OU system. We needed people who liked to brawl and who hated both Nazis and rich fucks. And if that's the kind of people you need, that's the kind of people you will get. Many fit the image of a stereotypical macho, that's true: street brawlers from the suburbs, hooligans, skinheads. When we started the OU system, I was part of the Southern Capital Commando.[6] We had a telephone list with forty people who all lived along the commuter train line to Södertälje: kickers and immigrant kids who hated Nazis and the rich.[7] Once, we did an action together with AFA. AFA showed up with fifteen people, we with ninety. That was only possible because of the OU system.

What was the "RF spirit"?

1: Stylish, militant.

2: Yes, style was important. Our slogan was: "No class, only style!"

1: But that wasn't about the clothing …

2: Partly.

1: Anyway, the clothes had to be whole and clean. Not like in the autonomous left! No, but seriously: "RF spirit" meant to have the class consciousness that the rest of the left was lacking. The autonomous left only started to talk about class again because of us. AFA didn't talk about class, SUF certainly didn't, and all those websites that existed, Motkraft or Yelah, they wrote about autonomous women's groups, animal rights, what have you, but not class. "No class, only style!" meant we would fight for a classless society and not care about anything else but style! Antifascism was important because the Nazis posed a threat to working-class unity. Besides, they were easy targets. The RF spirit meant that we were the vanguard of the working class. When I joined RF, I felt that I was spearheading the class struggle. We were here to fight the class's enemies.

And you felt that no other group was doing that?

1: That's right, I felt that no other group was doing that.

2: At least not in the same way, not even close.

1: I had experiences from the Revolutionary Communist Youth and the Communist Party.

2: Boo!

1: Whatever, you anarchist troll. Anyway, as I said, I felt that I was part of the working-class vanguard. We were uncompromising and bashed up those who we felt deserved it: Nazis and bourgeois fuckers.[8] If we had to, we visited them at their homes. We filmed the CEO of Busslink, because he had filmed his employees. We left garbage outside the house of Annie Lööf.[9] We hoped that others would wake up soon! To some degree, we succeeded. We radicalized parts of the autonomous left: AFA began to talk about class, and SUF as well. Varis in Finland was heavily influenced by us—I was there giving lectures.[10]

2: You told them about home visits.

1: I heard that RF shirts were sold in Germany. We inspired people. Maybe not the average Swedish worker, or the woman working twelve-hour shifts in a nursing home before returning to her housing estate apartment to cry, maybe not them. But we fought for them. We went looking for their boss if he was an asshole.

Okay, summarize the RF spirit in a few words!

1: Working-class vanguard, spearheading the class struggle, acting in the interests of the class. Antifascism was an easy way to come closer to that goal.

2: I agree with this to a certain extent, but it was also about an "us versus them" mentality. In the beginning, it was mainly us versus the many enemies we had on the left, because we didn't do what they wanted us to do. We didn't run, we fought, even if we were three against fifteen. That was an important part of the RF spirit: We were not like the others, and we were damn proud of it.

1: Articles like the one in Yelah strengthened that sentiment, and so did the fact that we could summon ninety people if necessary. In those moments, the class seemed unconquerable. I still see myself as part of RF.

What was the significance of Red Action for RF?

2: To be well clad! Red Action and the book *No Retreat* were a huge source of inspiration for us.[11] *No Retreat* was one of the first books that new members got to read. Red Action also fought against the rest of the left and took things into their own hands. They came from the working class and recruited in fish markets and ports.

1: RF was inspired by Red Action but also by antifa groups from other countries. In Red Action, we liked the Britishness, the culture, they spoke a lot about the working class. And the Red Action founders looked very similar to the RF founders, old skinheads. We traveled to England and hung out with them, experienced comrades. We talked a lot about Ireland with them too, which was an important topic for RF, especially in the beginning.

2: Why was that, actually?

1: Because of Red Action. They had put us in touch with Marian Price, who had been force-fed in a British prison.[12] She came to Stockholm to speak at Kafé 44.[13] Red Action was influential on RF in many ways, with regard to both class politics and antifascism. Two former members came for an event at the Community Hall in Skarpnäck, in southern Stockholm. A hundred and fifty people showed up and talked class politics all evening. *No Retreat* was sort of a bible for RF. Laugh if you want, but *everyone* had to read the book—and love it! We were not attracted by any of the leftist groups in Sweden, we wanted to be a working-class organization, we were into class struggle and union organizing. Our reference points were Red Action and *No Retreat*, not sexism or LGBTQ+. Our message was simple: "Punch the Nazi in the face, and punch the bourgeois motherfucker in the face!" They were our enemies. That message hit home with a lot of people.

How would you describe the political education in RF?
1: In Stockholm, we had quite a few reading circles. We even got money for that from ABF.[14] During the final years, we were able to gather forty people. Political education was important. We encouraged all RF locals to organize programs, both for members and the folks from the Operative Units.

"We Challenged Their Social Norms and Everything They Stand For"

There exist minutes from the first (of two) nationwide RF meetings in 2006, which help us better understand the collective identity of RF. This identity was formed during the organization's first years in Gothenburg. At the 2006 meeting, it was summarized thus:

> In order to understand where we find ourselves today, and why we are gathered here, we need to know our history and our background. The basic ideas and values of RF were created during this history. We are proud of it, and everybody here shall know about it.
>
> RF was founded by five people who were tired of being ostracized by the autonomous left. We had the burning desire to change the world, but the left's so-called activism frustrated us—to the point where working in any of the existing leftist groups no longer was an option.

I was allowed to look at the minutes from the 2006 meeting, which aren't available in any official archive. Among other things, the minutes include a list of problems that the RF founders associated with the autonomous left:

- politics is no priority
- internal conflicts aren't dealt with
- partying is more important than struggling
- for people who do not belong to the white middle class, who do not listen to a certain kind of music, who do not dress in a certain way, and who do not express themselves in a certain way, there is no place

- militant comrades are not valued, even though plenty of lip service is paid to militancy
- groups demand nothing of their members, which leads to a lack of politics and half-heartedness among the membership
- plenty of sexists, racists, hypocrites, and assholes

The following paragraph summarizes how RF wanted to be different:

> We wanted to focus on political struggle and invite everyone to work with us who shared that focus. We were welcome neither in the Revolutionary Communist Youth nor in AFA nor in SUF. We didn't fit into these groups because our mere existence posed a threat to them. We challenged their social norms and everything they stand for. We were full of energy, ready to do anything. We had a strong desire to change society. The work of other political groups didn't impress us. We knew that we could do it better. Our political consciousness was stronger. It seemed absurd to join groups that got in the way of real political activism and demanded nothing of their members.

In line with the interviews conducted for this book, this quote emphasizes that RF wanted to add something new to the left instead of reproducing dominant and hegemonic leftist culture. RF chose its own methods and strategies. The organization was more militant than AFA and used new forms of propaganda. The minutes from the nationwide meeting of 2006 prove that this was at the heart of the organization—something that every new member needed to be aware of.

The Critique Continues

We have sketched the critique that RF had of the autonomous left as well as the critique that the autonomous left had of RF. We'll stick with the latter a little longer and focus on three aspects: drugs, masculinity, and violence.

1. *Drugs*

RF was repeatedly criticized from within the left for members consuming vast amounts of alcohol and drugs, and also for members selling drugs. The critique was often exaggerated. Some RF members did make money by selling drugs, but the organization regularly discussed the negative consequences of alcohol and drug consumption for the working class. It was always prohibited to consume alcohol or drugs during actions. And next to the members who consumed—and, in some cases, sold—alcohol and drugs privately, there were also straight-edge members who never did. During certain periods, straight edge had a strong presence in RF, both in Gothenburg and Stockholm as well as Örebro.

In 2006, RF prohibited any sale of alcohol to other members and at fundraising events. Drugs weren't allowed to be sold to fellow members either. Alcohol was regarded as a legal drug that wasn't to be treated differently than illegal drugs. The minutes from the meeting where this decision was made read as follows:

> Alcohol has damaging effects on a lot of people. It is a huge social problem with thousands of victims every year. Most violent crimes and murders are committed by people who are under the influence of alcohol. RF refuses to support an industry that contributes to society's decay.

The prohibition of alcohol sales at fundraisers meant that RF needed to come up with creative solutions to raise funds. One of the most original ideas was the highly popular nude calendar that RF printed annually from 2006 to 2009. Each month sported the image of a masked RF member naked or sparsely clad, often with a baseball bat, brass knuckles, or something similar.

A complete ban on selling drugs was also discussed within RF. But in the end, only sales to fellow members were banned. The reason was that some members claimed they had no other means of earning an income. Another issue raised was whether the organization should really get involved in people's private lives. Finally, the argument was made that if there was a

Nude calendar, 2006.

complete ban on selling drugs, members could no longer work at Systembolaget either, as the morality of the state didn't trump personal morality.[15]

If the approach to drugs in RF appears contradictory, it's because there was no clear position within the organization. Some former members remember alcohol and drug use within the organization being widespread, especially during the early years, and they remember certain members selling drugs. Other members were straight edge. In short, lifestyles differed.

2. Masculinity

According to former RF members, there was a lot of discussion within the organization about why there were so few women who joined. Women never accounted for more than a few percent of the RF membership. The views on this differ among former members. Some think that the organization did too little to attract women. Others think that gender had no relevance. During RF's final years, the efforts to recruit women increased and women members were more visible in RF propaganda. Yet there were members who thought until the very end of RF that for a militant group active on the streets, diversity wasn't particularly important. We saw this view expressed in the interview "We Came from the Streets, We Didn't Need to Go There" (see pp. 11–22). In the interview "More Important Was That the Nazis Lost Control over the Streets Because of Us" (see pp. 23–32), the macho culture within RF was linked to the street fights that characterized RF's early years, as it might not have made RF particularly attractive to women. Other members concede that there was a macho culture in RF even apart from the street fighting, and that it should have been acknowledged as a problem and dealt with.

On the following pages, we will read more thoughts on this question by former RF members. We'll begin with a member who was in RF for eight years.

"You Can't Be Good at Street Fighting and Permanently Question Yourself"

Do you think that the critique of RF as too macho was justified?
Well, the macho thing ... if you consider what we did, then a macho element was inevitable. And it has an impact on the kind of people you attract. Plenty of things tie into it: how you dress, how you carry yourself, how you talk. At some point, it all becomes a self-fulfilling prophecy: You have a certain membership, and you'll attract people who fit that membership. I think we could have changed some of the internal culture, but to get rid of the macho element completely? Considering what we did? Impossible. You can't be good at street fighting and permanently question yourself, that doesn't work. As a result, you'd be a worse street fighter. Look at the members who hung out with hooligans,

or—maybe even worse—the ones who became criminals. They were the most brutal, and, truth be told, sometimes it sucked being around them. They were extremely macho, and at the same time very insecure boys. It should have not gone as far as it did in their cases, but again, to completely avoid that element would have been impossible.

But even if violence was central, compared to hooligans and criminals, you had a political purpose. Was there no political filter mitigating the machismo?
Yes, there was, and I would say that, for the most part, the vibes within the organization were okay. But there certainly was a stronger macho element than in other leftist groups. If you had brought kids from the Young Left to us, I don't think they would have felt very comfortable. I feel that people in RF were listening when you had personal problems or doubts, but overall things were always pretty rough. I think most activists, especially today's activists, wouldn't have been put off.

"That Experience Was Very Liberating and Empowering"

Many former members are of the opinion that the vibes within RF differed from other leftist groups, but not that much from regular society. In the following interview, a person who was an RF member for ten years explains that in RF personal relationships were more important than theory:

What's your take on the macho critique of RF?
I never felt reduced to my gender in RF. I have never been in social circles, not before and not after, where I felt as much on equal terms with anyone else as I did in RF. All members were the same, all were met with the same exceptions, and that was it. We were a collective, not men or women. This is one of the most important experiences I took with me from RF. I was active in a context where I was not defined by my gender, while that happens all the time otherwise. That experience was very liberating and empowering, and I have

been able to carry the strength I got from it with me since. I will always be grateful to RF for that.

But then, why did so few women join RF?
I think a lot had to do with how the organization presented itself. Many members had no political schooling, they were not socialized in the left. They appeared crude, and it might have been off-putting to women.

But wasn't that a problem?
Yes and no. It would have probably been better had more women joined RF, but if you had changed the organization only to attract more women, you would have likely lost others.

But aren't you suggesting that there was a vibe in the organization that wasn't particularly attractive to women?
Yes, but you must not forget the negative reputation that RF had within the left. During the final years, the membership of women increased. And, just to be clear, it's not like you have all that many women in other leftist groups either, or in politics in general.

"I'd Rather Cruise with an RF Chick than with Ten Barflies"

Various former RF members say that the macho critique of RF was strongest during the early years. Later, it subsided for two reasons: first, RF moved closer to the autonomous left; second, there was more understanding within the autonomous left of the conditions that RF members came from—conditions that weren't typical for leftist activists, which explained differences in conduct and language. But the macho critique of RF never ceased entirely. The following excerpt is from an interview with a person who was an RF member for five years:

Did you find the macho critique of RF justified?
RF was as macho as it had to be. I suppose violence in itself is macho: You want others to be scared of you, and you act

tough. But I never felt that RF was excluding people. I also don't think that RF was macho in a silly way, with "cool rides" and "hot chicks" and such, that would have been macho without any relevance. But with regard to appearing tough, yes, that was a macho ideal. Still, I never found the critique articulated in a just way. It came from people who had no clue. They knew nothing about RF. And they couldn't know anything, they weren't members. From the outside, RF might have appeared to be a bunch of crazy dudes not wanting to interact with anyone else. I get that. But there's a good RF quote: "I'd rather cruise with an RF chick than with ten barflies." It was all about being able to trust your companions, gender didn't matter.

What kind of impact did the violence have on you personally?
Violence wasn't a big thing for us, it was just a tool. We joked about it a lot. When violence is part of your everyday life, then humor is a good way of dealing with it. But underneath that, of course, you must not forget that violence is very serious. To keep a balance is not always easy, but we walked that line.

Did RF members stick to using violence only in a political context?
The honest answer is no. But me personally, I didn't witness much violence in other contexts.

Because you didn't drink and do drugs?
Yes, shout out to the Eskilstuna crew! We didn't do any of that. We all came from the hardcore scene and were straight edge. So for us, this was no problem. But, yes, other members could get violent outside of politics when they had too much to drink. Yet I didn't have the impression that alcohol and drugs were a huge problem in RF.

The following excerpt is from an interview with a person who was in RF during the final two years:

"No class struggle without women's struggle."

Was there a romanticization of violence in RF? Was RF too macho?

Many of the commonly held prejudices against RF weren't true. But some were: RF was very male, very macho, very violent, and members had a characteristic style, no one can deny that. Was that good or bad? Hard to say. But I would claim that every militant political organization has a complicated relationship to violence. Gender doesn't really play into it. I was very close to two of the women in RF. We shared the same political analysis, the same understanding of fascism, and the same understanding of violence. To associate violence with one gender only is also problematic.

You mean it's sexist?

If you claim that only men engage in violence and that women never ever do that, then I think it's sexist, yes. When you look at political history, it's full of militant women. The suffragettes bombed buildings in London while fighting for the right to vote, even if today that's swept under the rug. One of the very last RF leaflets focused on how militant women were written out of history. We distributed it before March 8. Two women from RF wrote it and complained that they were being made invisible every time the organization was accused of being macho.

Did you train street fighting? It wasn't a recognized martial art at the time, and it's still not well known as such today.

We were raised in the RF spirit, which distinguished us from the rest of the left.

What does that mean?
It means that you were convinced of your strength, as an individual and as a group. You had a kind of self-confidence that you didn't find elsewhere in the left. When I became a member, a comrade told me, "You do not need to be a martial arts expert. All you need is a useful weapon and a cool head." That was the RF spirit: You were certain that no one could harm you, you felt invincible.

But the RF nostalgia also exaggerates the violence. There were militant activists outside of RF too. It wasn't the violence as such that made RF unique, it was the aura of RF, an aura that groups like AFA didn't have. That gave you the upper hand psychologically. The RF label alone made the Nazis shit their pants.

3. *Violence*

The violence used by RF is hard to separate from the macho critique. There had never been a group in the Swedish left as militant as RF. But RF's reputation was only partly related to the violence itself—a very important aspect was how the violence was communicated. RF uploaded videos from street fights and home visits as well as pictures and written reports. Propaganda was important for RF. AFA could be downplayed by the fascists; they rarely claimed responsibility for actions, and the fascists could even claim that the network didn't really exist. With regard to RF, that was impossible. RF always documented their actions and took responsibility for them. Several former members interviewed for this book said that they joined RF because of the videos they had seen online. RF's reputation was far superior to that of AFA, and RF's propaganda was the most important reason why the group attracted international attention as well.

"Pretty Rough"

RF had its own jargon. Members were called "RF material," and there was plenty of talk about the "RF spirit." The terms were meant to emphasize that RF was different from the rest of the Swedish left. RF embraced that role, yet it had originally come from RF being rejected by the rest of the left. In order to get a better understanding of this dynamic, it helps to shed light on the autonomous left in Sweden as a social movement.

We use "social movement" mostly as an umbrella term for individuals, groups, and organizations that share a set of principles and become active through more or less formalized networks. Usually, they have a common enemy and develop a collective identity.

The autonomous movement in Sweden (which I use as a synonym for the "autonomous left") can be described as an extraparliamentary movement sharing socialist values. It reaches from communists to anarchists. The common enemy is class society, and the common struggle against capitalism is the driving force.

RF was part of the autonomous left in Sweden, but grudgingly. Within the autonomous left, RF had a strong, unique identity. The main pillar of this identity was RF's critique of the rest of the left: middle-class kids, too much lifestyle, politics being treated as a mere hobby. RF explicitly set itself apart from this culture (or "subculture," as they put it), which was also a statement: If the left was serious about class politics, there would be working-class people in its ranks.

RF was founded on the basis of two convictions: one, the Nazis on the streets had to be defeated; two, the autonomous left was inept, not least because it had no class analysis. These convictions defined RF until it dissolved in 2015.

RF GAINS TERRITORY

"

AFA had a wide network and had to take care of all sorts of things. They were also more open—pretty much anyone could join AFA. But that also meant responsibility. Had we had forty confused teenagers with us, we would have been responsible for them too—and probably would have been distracted from our main task.

MEMORY "FOR US, THIS IS NOTHING NEW, BUT MANY OF THEM REALIZE FOR THE FIRST TIME IN THEIR LIVES THAT THE COPS WILL NEVER BE ON OUR SIDE."

"This story should really be told by many people. Each of them had their own door, and each door had its own story.

I don't remember the hour, but a friend and I had just returned from downtown to our neighborhood when the phone rang. Nazis were harassing a protest at the detention center in Märsta organized by a migrant justice group. As usual, the cops didn't care, and the people at the protest did not feel safe. The phone rang constantly as my friend and I headed back into town. We were in a hurry, since we needed to get to Märsta as quickly as possible; there was no time to gather a bigger group. This is how it all unfolded ...

When we get on the commuter train to Märsta, we are about ten people. During the trip, we receive a constant flow of information. The last thing we hear is that the Nazis are waiting for us at the Märsta train station, apparently twenty-five to thirty of them. We are ready and convinced that we'll just roll over them.

Coming into the station at Märsta, we split into two groups, each waiting by its own door. The groups stand tight, and we are ready to storm the platform as soon as the doors open. We do, and run straight into a line of cops. The cops throw us against the wall or on the ground. The Nazis stroll by with cops as escorts. The officers put the Nazis on the train we just arrived on and order them to go to Stockholm. Once the train has left the station, we are released. We then make our way to the detention center.

There, the cops fuck up, as usual. They tell the organizing group of the protest that it's time for them to go to the station and to take the next train back to Stockholm as well. The organizing group objects to that, as they are expecting the Nazis to wait for them somewhere along the train line. But the cops don't budge and force them to take the train. We ride with them. There are also plenty of regular passengers on the train, including elderly people and families with small children. I recall at least two prams. Some of the regular passengers ask the cops to come along. They refuse.

As soon as the train has left the station, we hear that the Nazis are waiting for us at a station close by. They have collected hundreds of rocks from the train tracks. We quickly discuss what to do and spread out across the train, two or three of us covering one door each. A good comrade and I get the last door. We decide that as soon as the doors open, we will jump out, grab some rocks, and get into a rock-throwing battle with the fashes—provided they aren't right in front of our door!

They aren't, and we get to throw rocks their way. But it still makes me mad that we weren't able to do more. When the doors open, the Nazis are in the middle of the platform, as they don't know what our strategy is. As my comrade and I throw rocks at them, we see the Nazis throw rocks through the windows of the train. Luckily, our comrades are able to keep them from getting on the train. Some of us try to pull a Nazi who has fallen to the ground into the train, but his buddies manage to save him.

I will never forget the moment when the train left the station: None of us is seriously injured, but the other passengers are panic-stricken. Some cry hysterically. All of the windows are broken, and I have a vivid memory of shards of glass covering one of the prams. The Nazis are still on the platform as we leave.

The cops stop the train at the next station and arrest everyone whose personal information they collected in Märsta, meaning: us. They show no sympathy or offer any help to the other passengers. For us, this is nothing new, but many of them realize for the first time in their lives that the cops will never be on our side.

—Written by a former RF Stockholm member[1]

Who Controls Territory?

Times were changing. In the early 2000s, Nazis still controlled vast areas of the inner city of Stockholm, especially around the helipad that appears in numerous interviews and written memories in this book. But by 2007, the attacks on the Nazis started to pay off. They were losing control over these areas. They still met at the helipad, but they no longer posed the same danger. In Gothenburg, it was similar. You no longer met Nazis in the city who openly displayed their ideology.

Instead, it was RF and other antifascists who had taken control over significant areas. For example, no fascist dared to enter the old working-class neighborhood of Södermalm in Stockholm, because they knew that it wouldn't be beneficial to their health. Thanks to defectors and informants, RF had access to the fascists' internal communication, so they knew that the

Nazis warned each other about visits to Södermalm. So looking for Nazis there was a waste of time: They didn't show.

RF's success in reclaiming territory could not be explained by technically superior street fighting alone. Strategy was more important than skill. Most important, perhaps, was the "RF spirit." The Little League, for example, was able to teach much older Nazis a lesson, because they heeded the RF doctrine: "Never hesitate! Never retreat! Always punch first! Be with comrades you trust a hundred percent! No one is left behind!"

Since RF members fought Nazis constantly, they developed routines and turned into tight-knit groups. This applied to all RF locals. It also meant that an RF member was at home in any local. When an RF Gothenburg member joined an action in Stockholm, they could feel a hundred percent safe, and vice versa. A strong sense of unity permeated the entire organization.

One of the biggest threats for RF was Info-14. Info-14 ran the biggest Nazi website during the early 2000s and was active on the streets as well. In 2007, they wanted to reclaim the area around the helipad, intending to turn it into a fascist nest once again.

The War Against the Free Nationalists

In Gothenburg, a group by the name of Gothenburg's Free Nationalists (GFN) was founded in 2004 in the suburb of Torslanda. They put up stickers, attended Nazi festivals, and so on. Sometimes they beat up Nazi skinheads, whom they didn't like. Mostly, though, they attacked leftists.

This led to the "War Against the Free Nationalists," as RF called it. Free Nationalists were a trend in the Nazi scene at the time.[2] In 2008, Info-14 initiated a nationwide network under that name. GFN became part of it, adapting its name to "Free Nationalists Gothenburg." Since they already were an established group, they remained at the center of Sweden's Free Nationalist movement. In Gothenburg, they dominated the fascist scene, which was why RF had to pay particular attention to them, as detailed in the following interview:

The Free Nationalists were a new thing in Gothenburg. My impression was that they were Nazi survivors of the battles of the early 2000s. Most other fascists in Gothenburg at the time were hardly worth mentioning: a blend of baby Nazis and aging skinheads from the 1990s. In the early 2000s, there were still many fascists, even if they were undisciplined and not well organized. Then, growing age and relentless antifascist resistance killed them off. Night patrols, physical attacks, property damage—their cars were a popular target—showed results. But with GFN, there were fascists in town again who didn't just lie down but were ready to fight.

In the beginning, GFN was nothing but a street crew, many of them from Torslanda, a predominantly white suburb. They chose the easiest targets, people with keffiyehs and such. But they soon understood that we posed the biggest threat to them, and they began to target us specifically. I had the windows of my apartment smashed several times. When we met them in town, they didn't run. They weren't as strong as us, but they stood their ground.

Otherwise, there isn't much to say about their activism. They went to Nazi rallies and festivals and put up stickers. At the Nazi events, they apparently beat up skinheads every so often. I think they saw them as embarrassing remnants of a bygone era. If they had a political program in the beginning at all, it was fighting antifascists. Then, they grew closer to Info-14, which wanted to build a nationwide network of Free Nationalists. GFN even changed its name for that, but nothing much came of it, so they went back to the old name. The connections to Info-14 also became weaker—or they ceased entirely, I'm not sure. But I'm pretty sure they were the only Free Nationalists still around after the complete network failure. They had probably become a bit more ideological due to the collaboration with Info-14, whose program was a bit more advanced than just fighting antifascists and attending Nazi festivals. But you didn't notice it much. After the network failure, GFN pretty much was the same gang they had been before.

Can you tell us more about the "War Against the Free Nationalists"?
There was plenty of violence. I can't even tell you how often we fought with them. It included bigger brawls, when groups of us met in the city, and smaller, targeted attacks. There were also home visits. GFN members never felt safe in the city, which was good. But their biggest weakness was their decadence: tons of drugs and many internal conflicts, including relationship dramas. Members hit on other members' sisters, stuff like that. Apparently, one of them was responsible for another member's sister overdosing. Drugs were their Achilles' heel. In the early 2010s, I ran into one of their former leaders, and I would not have recognized him had a friend not pointed him out. Only two or three years earlier, it would have been impossible for me to miss him, but he no longer looked the same because of all the drugs he was doing. They also had problems with the Wisemen, the hooligan firm of IFK. At first, they benefited from their connections to the Wisemen, because they provided access to people who weren't particularly political but happy to beat up leftists and antifas, especially from RF, because RF was associated with GAIS. Eventually, though, the Wisemen bosses got fed up with it and told their members that they had to pick either football or politics—and most of them picked football.

During the War Against the Free Nationalists, RF Gothenburg sometimes collaborated with AFA Gothenburg. But when the Free Nationalist network collapsed, RF and AFA ran into tensions. Partly, it might have been old conflicts resurfacing, but RF specifically complained about the lack of financial assistance from AFA. AFA did many fundraisers and had good international connections, which meant that they had a fair bit of money. RF was questioning what AFA did with the money. RF members felt that they were more active. To them, that meant both that they didn't have as much time for fundraising and that they would put AFA's money to better use. In short, RF's opinion was that if

"For the defense of our class! Put an end to the fascists!"

AFA was serious about wanting to support militant antifascism, they should give at least some of the money to RF, since no one was practicing militant antifascism at their level. And RF was always short of money. So when AFA, after the War Against the Free Nationalists, gave a significant amount of money to SUF but not to RF, it did not go down well. A former RF Gothenburg member will elaborate on this in an interview below.

RF also accused the AFA research unit of withholding important information from them, for example the addresses of active fascists. This critique, too, was based on RF's activist orientation. RF felt that it only made sense to gather information about Nazis if the information was put to practical use. Gathering information for its own sake made no sense. The way that AFA handled this confirmed for RF that they were as self-centered and elitist as other leftist groups, and the conflict with AFA confirmed for RF that they had no friends within the left.

The relationship between RF and AFA was always strained despite occasional collaboration. This made it difficult to build a strong, united antifascist movement.

MEMORY THE BATTLE OF SOLNA TORG[3]

"One of our informants from within the fascist movement had sent us interesting information. NSF and the Free Nationalists held a common rally in Solna, near Stockholm, and we received the places and the hours of their preparatory meetings that day. NSF was stronger throughout Sweden than the Free Nationalists, but in Stockholm, the latter dominated the Nazi scene back then. They organized the march in Salem and concerts in the name of the Yellow Cross, and they ran Info-14.[4] NSF was also less present on the streets. All of that meant that we focused on the prep meeting of the Free Nationalists; we'd attend to NSF if time allowed.

We began with our own preparations a few weeks before the event. We needed scouts, a meeting place before the action, an assembly point for when we were done with it, and an attack plan. We also needed to make travel arrangements for the comrades from outside of Stockholm. Unfortunately, it was quite far from the center of Solna to the subway and commuter train stations. It posed a challenge, because you want to remain undetected until the scouts give you the green light to attack. But we found a meeting place where it was relatively easy to disappear into the crowd. Every member received the relevant information: place, time, the clothes to be worn, and the weapons to be brought. As far as weapons were concerned, we only had one rule at the time: no knives.

When the day came, I could feel it in my entire body. It was just like before a hooligan fight; the adrenaline was pumping. But this was no hooligan fight. We had no unwritten rules about not kicking people on the ground, about not using weapons, and so forth. Okay, there's an exception to every rule, and sometimes hooligans, too, kick people on the ground and bring along weapons. But what's an exception for them was a rule for us. Strategically, it was simply unwise not to kick a Nazi lying on the ground. Besides, it is almost impossible not to do it when adrenaline gets mixed with hate. The thing with the weapons is merely a tactical question. It was never about killing Nazis, but each action had a specific goal: You wanted to chase them from the street, disrupt an event, break their morale.

Back to the day in Solna. Again, I felt it in my body. I had selected the clothes I would be wearing days before, so now I just had to put them on. I was way too excited to eat breakfast; I just wanted to get out of the house. I had not been involved in the planning, but I knew that both the fascists and us would get backup from other cities. If our timing wasn't perfect, we risked facing a much bigger group of opponents than expected. After all, they had mobilized for a rally. Fuck it!

I got way too restless at home, so I left early, together with some comrades. On a day like this, there was always a chance to meet a Nazi lost on his way to the rally. But that day we didn't, and so we eventually took the subway to our meeting place. From there, we were sent to a park, where we sat down on the grass. More and more comrades showed up. We sat in small groups and tried to act as inconspicuously as possible, which became increasingly difficult, since our numbers grew significantly. Then we got a message from the scouts. About twenty Nazis had gathered at their very own meeting place. It was time to attack!

Each group started to move. All in all, we were eighty people now. We had to walk for ten minutes without being detected. On a Saturday morning in Solna, this wasn't easy.

The closer we got to our destination, the more obvious it became who the hungriest among us were. I was at the head of the pack. Now we were very close! The banter around me stopped; everyone was quiet and focused. My heart was beating fast, and my legs were shaking. I knew this would stop the second we attacked. There was only a small hill left, one road to cross, and then we'd need to follow a small pathway through apartment buildings to the square. We needed to be careful a little longer still! Any premature move could have spoiled everything. The situation was tense. You never know what is going to happen when eighty people full of adrenaline and hate get ready to launch an attack. We, who were at the top, slowed down to allow all comrades to catch up.

Right when we reached the top of the hill, a police patrol came around the corner. We were in a parking lot; someone must have called them. There were two cops in the car with dogs. They got out and brought the dogs with them. We at the front hesitated for a moment, unsure about what to do. Proceed or turn around? Within an instant, the cops detained two of us. We knew it wouldn't be long before their colleagues would turn up.

Hail horizontal organizing! The comrades at the back reacted instantly when they saw the cops and took a different route. All of us were able to follow them except for the five of us who were up front. Fuck, this was not supposed to happen! We knew that as soon as more cops arrived, our day would be done. But the cops present did not have full control of the situation yet. They were only two. All I needed was for one of them to be distracted for a moment, so I could duck behind some vehicles and get the hell out. I managed!

Unfortunately, I was now at the back of the pack. Not happy about that at all! I always want to see what's going on, be active. I want to be right at the front! We walked through another park and still had the road to cross to get to the square. We knew that the Nazis were now only fifty yards away, assembling behind a food truck. If they had scouts, they should already be able to see us. We started to run. I had made it back to the front. We crossed a bus station and saw the Nazis. Their numbers had grown to about thirty-five. Now they saw us too.

As usual, they had brought glass bottles in case of an attack. The bottles were pouring down on us. We spread out and advanced bit by bit. I was on the right; the Nazis retreated toward the left. Fuck, wrong side! Soon, fists were flying and we took control of the situation, even though the Nazis threw furniture from a restaurant terrace. I grabbed one of the chairs and ran toward the wannabe Vikings. One of them, a big fellow, was brave enough to stand his ground, throwing punches. I was aiming for him. My plan was to throw the chair at him, make him lose his balance, and then throw him to the ground. I approached, threw the chair—and he caught it with one hand! It was too late to change my plans, so I kept charging toward him while he raised the chair, ready to smash it on my head. All I could think was, "Damn, this is going to hurt!" when, right before he could drop the chair, he was attacked by a comrade with a broken bottle.

Most Nazis had escaped to a staircase leading to an inner yard. The ones who hadn't were in bad shape. Those in charge of our attack decided that it was time to bail, as there would soon be cops everywhere.

—Written by a former RF Stockholm member

MEMORY "WHEN WE TELL HIM, 'IT'S ALL RIGHT, IT'S A NAZI,' HE TURNS AROUND AND CALMLY WALKS BACK TO HIS BUS."

"I don't recall the exact year, but we could not, under any circumstances, allow the National Democrats to hold their general meeting undisturbed. Let me start with a disclaimer you've heard many times before: All you'll get is my perspective. I'm sure there are plenty more.

We had received information about ND meeting with skinheads and other fascists at the commuter train station in Solna to travel to Södertälje.[5] Apparently, this would be a group of about a hundred people. We weren't too psyched about that, because for us it was a hard weekend to mobilize. AFA Stockholm and quite a few of us were in Germany—I don't remember why, but riot tourism was big at the time.

In the end, we were fifteen experienced and reliable comrades and ten less experienced and perhaps less reliable ones. We figured that was enough to spoil their shit. We'd had fun with the ND fools all year, and we approached this action like any other: fast, hard, straightforward. But we realized at the meeting place that the inexperienced folks didn't have the RF spirit. In hindsight, we should have sent them home, but we took them along for the ride on the commuter train instead. We were well armed and our self-confidence was sky-high.

Before we arrived in Södertälje, we heard from our scouts that the Nazi crowd was as big as expected, and that they had crates of glass bottles with them. Everyone who knows the commuter train station in Solna knows the tunnel leading to the bridge from where you descend to the tracks. This is how I recall things unfolding …

As always, we remind each other that we have to stick together. As always, there are some who don't. One of us runs into the tunnel ahead of everyone else, only to return a few moments later with blood running down his face. As soon as he stepped into the tunnel, he was pummeled by bottles.

On the other side of the tunnel, we can see the bridge, which is full of Nazis. They make a ruckus and seem prepared for battle. We try to get through the tunnel together, but we can't make it through the hail of bottles. We expect the Nazis to run through the tunnel and attack us at any moment. But no one comes. And, suddenly, they are out of bottles. Now they just stand on the other side of the tunnel and scream. It seems that they only feel safe at a respectable distance. I run into the tunnel with two comrades, and others are following. We have basically cleared the tunnel before we meet a Nazi. He is a bit braver than his pals, but we punch him to the ground in no time.

After that, I don't recall many details—my memory fails me. But we go wild in the tunnel. The Nazis don't pose any problems. They are cowardly and scared. Their "resistance" consists of pure panic. They have no clue what they are doing. We flatten one after the other, on occasion two at once. But we are too cautious and don't advance fast enough. We don't have full control over the situation. In hindsight, we should have just pushed forward. I'm sure the cowards would have run. And, indeed, when we reach the end of the tunnel, they have retreated and put a safe distance between themselves and us again. But we get a hold of two of them, and what follows says a lot about our cowardly opponents: None of them comes to help their pals, not even when they're on the ground with us gathered around them. A comrade who has a nightstick is trying to bash them over their heads with it, but he doesn't have enough space to swing it. Another comrade tells him, "Fuck their heads, take the kneecaps!"

Eventually, one of the cowards pulls himself together and showers everyone, including the two now unconscious Nazis on the ground, in tear gas. He is hit in the head by a rock and falls to the ground as well. When we hear the sirens of patrol cars, we bail. I hardly see anything because of the tear gas in my eyes.

On the following day, we read in the papers that the cops kettled and bused away eighty people. They found one person unconscious in the bushes, and quite a few had to be taken to the hospital. A Nazi who had been hit with a manhole cover had a fractured skull. Tragic—may he rest in peace! None of us got arrested, and only the overenthusiastic comrade who ran into the tunnel by himself needed a few stitches to put his face back together.

Days like these were days to celebrate. Nobody went home after the action. We knew that on a day like that, there might be more to come. By the time the ND meeting was reaching its end, we sent out scouts again. They informed us when the Nazis were heading for the commuter trains. The probable destination for most of them: Stockholm's central railway station. And so the story of that day continues ...

Ten of us are waiting there for the Nazis at the station. We all agree that we will not attack there but follow the Nazis to a better place. We know from experience that there is a disproportionate risk of getting arrested at the station.

When the commuter train arrives, we follow two Nazis to the subway. To honor the day, it's a pair of father and son, the father fifty years old, the son maybe thirty. In the subway, I take a seat opposite them. It's a surreal situation. They are completely unaware of what's awaiting them and reflect on the day, speaking, among other things, about the morning fight in Solna. My fingers are itching.

They debark at the Slussen subway station, still not a good place to attack. My comrades and I exchange looks that all ask the same question: "What now?" The Nazis are heading for the bus stop. One of us says, "We gotta take them now, otherwise we run out of options."

We get close, and right as they're leaving the station, the father is knocked down by a bottle to his head. The son tries to escape, but we are chasing him. For a moment I'm thinking, "Damn, the pig is getting away," but you're not running very fast in boots. I catch up with him, and he gets a bottle right in his face.

I don't wanna go into too much detail, but he gets it bad. Then a bus driver comes over and tells us to stop. When we tell him, "It's all right, it's a Nazi," he turns around and calmly walks back to his bus.

Father and son had to be taken to the hospital. And I was fascinated by how well Vanish works, even for blood stains.

—*Written by a former RF Stockholm member*

The Salem March

The Salem March was an annual event from 2000 to 2012. It was organized by people close to Info-14. Salem is a small community south of Stockholm. In 2012, the march was held in the inner city of Stockholm, probably because the number of participants in Salem had dwindled over the years. The reason for the march was a young fascist who had died of a stab wound during a confrontation with other youngsters on December 9, 2000. The Nazis celebrated him as a martyr. In the early 2000s, the Salem March was an important propaganda event for the far right.

But not only fascists came to Salem every year. Big protests were held against the march. In the beginning, they were organized by the autonomous left, together with socialist and social democratic organizations. The social democrats and some of the socialists pulled out after a few years, probably because of repeated clashes between antifascists and the Nazis, later also between antifascists and the police. Salem is a quaint town with single-family homes and three-story apartment buildings. For the local population, the march was a major disturbance.

In the following interview, a former member talks about the significance of the march for RF:

I think the march was important for RF. From 2005, we played an important role in the protests. RF members had been in Salem before, but then RF was still a small organization. I think the march brought us closer together. We met there every year without having to sit in endless meetings—the nationwide meetings we had could be quite tedious. In Salem, there was stuff to do. The event was important for other organizations as well, such as AFA. For us, it was a celebration. Leading up to the march, we distributed leaflets and chased Nazis. We had "night patrols" in Stockholm together with antifascists from the entire country. It was worth the effort. We always found Nazis, since they came to Salem from the entire country too. And after the patrols, we ate breakfast together!

You and other groups?
No. AFA's role in Salem was different. AFA hosted the international guests, coordinated the buses from Norway and Denmark, made sure they had all the information they needed, and food as well. They were also behind sabotaging the commuter train line, which made it very difficult for the Nazis to even get to Salem. We did different things.

You spoke of a "celebration" lasting several days. How important was the day of the march itself?
It was important too, of course.

Did you attack Nazis that day?
Yes, we bashed them up along the commuter train line, at the stations, and in the trains. We also smashed their cars. One year, the Little League erected a roadblock right as you enter Salem, and when they saw a Nazi car, they made sure they wouldn't go anywhere. But over time, these things became

more difficult because of the ever-increasing police presence. Eventually, you couldn't even see the Nazis anymore. That's when we started to fight the cops instead. It was good for our morale, it tied us together, but it wasn't really what we were there for. You had to be creative, throw smoke grenades on the train tracks, stuff like that. The goal was to disrupt the march. Most importantly, however, was to find Nazis in the evening and fuck them up.

Did you get fucked up too?
Us? Never. Couldn't happen when we were disciplined and organized.

Who were the Nazis behind the Salem March?
Info-14. They had a front group called the "Salem Fund." There was a lot of petty infighting. Some Nazis thought that Info-14 had too much power. One year, we managed to give the march's main organizer, Robert Vesterlund, two beatings on the same day, just before the march. We found him at two different places in Stockholm.

Can you say more about the Nazis' internal conflicts?
I don't know exactly what they quarreled about. Some probably had different ideas about the march, or they simply wanted to have more of a say. Meanwhile, the people from the Salem Fund were frustrated, because they had to do all the work. Since other fascists had little to say, they didn't help organize the march either. No distribution of leaflets or anything, they just showed up. The Salem Fund people distributed a newspaper every year, which made them an easy target for us. We only had to find out where the newspaper got distributed and could give them a good hiding.

In 2012, the march went through the old town of Stockholm, and that was the end of it. Did the march end because of the antifascist protests or because of the infighting among the fascists?

2012 was a fiasco. Maybe they would have continued otherwise. But very few people came that year, and they were attacked all day long. Even in their own videos, it is obvious that they could hardly move and were scared shitless. They had no idea what to do, it was total chaos. It was probably the last drop needed for the circus to end. But the fascist movement also went through a rough time.

You have talked about the meaning of the march for RF. How important was the march for the antifascist movement in general?
It brought people from all over the country together. You got to know new antifascists, and you made connections. I think this was very important.

Let us take a broader perspective: Kungsträdgården, Kärrtorp, Limhamn—antifas resisted militantly in all these places.[6] Since 2014, we haven't seen much of that. Do you think this is related to RF dissolving?
No, I don't think so. It was never an RF strategy to fight cops. We did it in Salem to disrupt the march. Apart from that, fighting the cops was of no interest to us. We wanted to bash up Nazis, far away from the cops. Our favorite would have been to give the Nazis a hiding at a train station and then disappear. Nobody wanted the cops around. We didn't like them, but we saw no point in fighting them. The Nazis were our target.

Did the same apply to other antifa groups? Or did they target cops as well?
There was no antifa group that had fighting cops as an explicit strategy. Primarily, they all wanted to bash up Nazis. But there were differences in how they went about it. Take the example of Salem: AFA had a wide network and had to take care of all sorts of things. They were also more open—pretty much anyone could join AFA. But that also meant responsibility. Had we had forty confused teenagers with us, we would

have been responsible for them too—and probably would have been distracted from our main task. We wanted to act with people we trusted, people who were RF members or in an Operative Unit. It doesn't matter how big your group is, but you must have the right people. We did our thing, others did theirs.

MEMORY THE COPS CONFUSE RF WITH NAZIS (AND NOT JUST ONCE)

"I can't recall all the details, but in Salem it was customary for the cops to chase antifascists through town. It was part of the protests, and everyone knew that. The hullabaloo was supposed to delay or, ideally, stop the march. But we had other priorities, and also local contacts. So while the cops acted tough, the leftists dealt with their trauma in the forest, and the Nazis froze their asses off, we sat in an apartment in Salem, discussed politics with some local residents, and ate cinnamon buns. Our job was usually done at that time, so we could relax. Then, we left Salem in peace and quiet, as if nothing had happened.

Our focus was always on the hours before and after the march. The spectacle of the march itself was of little interest to us. Sure, we were into doing actions. But to hide in the forest? No thanks.

There are many tales about RF. A common theme is the cops confusing us with Nazis. More than once did we end up in the same police van as them. One well-known tale is about the cops storming a subway train to arrest us but then dragging out innocent kids in keffiyehs, while paying us no intention. All because they were looking for "left-wing extremists."

Neither the Nazis nor the cops ever got RF. They didn't understand that we hang out with ordinary people. The public image of RF was shaped by all the trials—sometimes by trials where none of the accused even was an RF member.

But people like to create myths. They're not interested in regular everyday shit.

—*Written by a former RF Gothenburg member*

PUBLIC HUMILIATION OF THE SALEM FUND

The following originally appeared on www.revfront.org (November 16, 2005):

During the last few days, Robert Vesterlund's lackeys have bothered unsuspecting passersby at the Brommaplan subway station with the dirty propaganda of their pathetic Salem Fund. Since Stockholm's antifascists could not tolerate this, fifteen of them went to Bromma to help the department for city cleaning, to keep our proud capital tidy. The antifa unit consisted of members from RF and AFA along with independents.

In Bromma, we took care of fifteen Salem Fund fools in a proven and tested manner. Their pitiful performance was both entertaining and embarrassing. They had their dirty faces washed with pepper spray.

Unfortunately, Johnny Ström's impressive leadership qualities became obvious.[7] When attacked, the Salem Fund members demonstrated that they must have gone through rigorous training, including sprinting drills. When Johnny awakes in the hospital, he will be proud to know that his Aryan warriors excelled in the Swedish Nazis' favorite discipline: "100 meters—leave your Führer."

RF owes the Salem Fund some gratitude. Even if we disrupted the distribution of the newspaper, meeting you in connection with the *Salem Flame* indeed brought some much-appreciated light into this dark time of the year.[8]

Greetings from RF and the other participants!

PS: A cop got to taste a bit of pepper spray too. Poor fellow ...

NO CLASS, ONLY STYLE

“

If you are young and violence is a part of everyday life, then an organization such as RF could be extremely attractive. Or at least it was for me. Hard, uncompromising class struggle—there was a complete lack of it in the left at the time! I became an RF member because I was convinced of the strategic approach: You attack the Nazis where they feel safe, and you do it from a class-struggle angle. Brilliant!

MEMORY “THAT'S HOW WE TREATED STRIKEBREAKERS.”

“For some time, we served together with other organizations as a kind of muscle for the SAC, the syndicalist union—or at least in Stockholm, I don't know how it was in other locals. There was a blockade of a restaurant in the old town, Lilla Karachi, because SAC members had been treated badly by the owner. We stood out front and kept people from entering—not physically, but we could be intimidating if needed.

One day, a group came to have lunch. We got in their way. A slick fellow in designer clothes, maybe forty-five, seemed particularly bothered by a woman blocking his way. He started to get lippy and just as he was about to say, “You little bi—,” we unloaded on him and didn't hold back. His friends got some too. Then we left.

We were criticized for the violence by the SAC, but we

> didn't care. That's how we treated strikebreakers, especially when they called one of us a bitch.
>
> —*Told by a former RF Stockholm member*

"History Teaches Us That We Have Learned Nothing from History"

In 2005, RF decided to focus more on class politics. One reason was that the organization had been growing. Another was that fewer and fewer Nazis were on the streets, not least as a consequence of RF's activism. RF had carved out room to engage in other political activities. Class politics had, of course, always been important. For RF, fascism was a symptom of class society. Even if they considered defeating the fascists on the streets necessary, they knew that this alone would not lead to a classless society.

That RF saw a connection between capitalism and fascism was nothing out of the ordinary. This connection is emphasized by many groups on the left. But RF did not want to copy other groups; they wanted to adapt everything to their own goals. It was important for them to reach people who could otherwise easily fall victim to fascist propaganda, for example people in the suburbs. This was where most of the membership came from.

In an article titled "This Is Why We Fight Nazism," RF members stressed that they shared a working-class background with many fascists. That's why RF members saw fascism as a threat to working-class unity. Read an excerpt from the article, which appeared on www.revfront.org, below:

> It's important to emphasize that most fascists we are fighting come from the same class and the same socioeconomic background that we come from, especially in the bigger cities. Statistical data confirms this. They come from social groups that, just twenty years ago, still strongly identified with the left, but where fascism has had much success since. This underlines one of the biggest

dangers that fascism poses, and it explains why we have to fight it with all means necessary. But in order to do so, we must be able to reach the people of these social groups, often white, heterosexual, working-class men. If we don't, how can we claim to speak for everyone? How can we prevent the middle class from taking control over the political left? [...]

Words did not stop the Nazis the last time they came around, and words will not stop them this time either. The Nazis themselves confirm this. They laugh about pundits on TV and go on chasing and abusing leftists. They know that they have to control the streets in order not to lose their base. If we want to defeat fascism, we must defeat it where it derives its legitimacy from.

We are facing a historical dilemma. "History teaches us that we have learned nothing from history." That's exactly what happens if we downplay the fascist threat. In precisely that moment, the fascist movement will grow, gather new momentum, and assume that ordinary people will not challenge it.

We cannot afford to make the same mistake twice. The historical lesson is clear. Two things need to be combined in order to defeat the fascists: first, we need a clear political alternative; second, we must be ruthless.

This is why RF fights fascism without compromise—something that has led the media and the establishment to observe us very closely. We go to the bottom of fascism! We don't hate fascists because *Aftonbladet* or Mona Sahlin do.[1] Fuck *Aftonbladet* and Mona Sahlin! We hate fascists—and we fight them to our last man and our last woman—because fascists are a threat to us and our class interests. They stand in the way of creating a better world. Fascism has always despised, devalued, and deprived the working class, while entertaining itself with idiotic theories about the unity of "race" and "nation." Meanwhile,

"The working class always comes first."

> those who profit from the system reap the benefits of our labor. The political right is full of parasites.
>
> We fight fascism, and we fight the neoliberal system that might bring brownshirts to the streets of Sweden again.[2] Time is short. They are already marching in Salem.

The article "This Is Why We Fight Nazism" ties antifascism to class politics. It accuses fascism of splitting the working class. RF felt that the autonomous left in Sweden had lost sight of class politics, which also meant that discussions about fascism were stagnating. There was no theory to inform an effective political practice. For RF, theory without practice was worthless. They found it not surprising that the left no longer was a factor in working-class communities. They also found it not surprising that most leftist groups were dominated by folks from the middle class. RF members felt they had no place in these groups, and they didn't want a place there; they wanted to preserve their own working-class culture. In this sense, their refusal to be "politically correct" and adapt to the norms of the autonomous left was more than childish defiance. It was based on a positive class identity. RF hoped that this would allow them to attract more working-class people.

The interviews conducted for this book make it clear that RF was attractive to working-class people because RF's class politics were less compromised than those of other leftists. Many former members also believe that the violence the public associated RF with was helpful in advancing class politics, even if RF rarely used violence apart from its antifascist activism. RF protested laws limiting workers' rights, and they got a fair bit of attention for taking down the website jobbjakt.se, where people could offer jobs to whoever was willing to take the lowest pay for them.[3] A visit to the company's CEO was enough to put an end to it.

Occupations: Aspuddsbadet and Rinkebyhuset

In 2009, two buildings were occupied in Stockholm with RF involvement: a public bath in the Aspudden neighborhood and an administrative building in the suburb of Rinkeby. The occupation in Aspudden was more successful—perhaps because RF was the driving force behind it.

Aspuddsbadet

Aspudden lies in southern Stockholm. Aspuddsbadet was built in 1919 for the local population's personal hygiene. In the early twentieth century, few apartments in the working-class neighborhoods of Stockholm had their own bathrooms.

In 2009, the Stockholm city council declared its intention to demolish the public bath. Since some RF members lived in the neighborhood, RF Stockholm got involved in the protests against the demolition. RF didn't care all that much about whether the site would house a bath or, as the city council proposed, a kindergarten, but they wanted to defend a building that was of historical importance to the local working class.

The occupation of the building was RF's idea, and RF was responsible for carrying it out. During the occupation, there were meetings held in the building, and film screenings as well as concerts were organized. RF also made sure that "lifeguards" were on site every night to prevent the police from raiding the bath.[4]

In the following interview, an RF member involved in the occupation talks about RF's role:

> Aspuddsbadet was an old bath for the working class of the neighborhood. It opened in the early twentieth century. People from Aspudden still went there to take baths. There were many regulars, and the building had a derelict charm. Eventually, the city council decided to tear it down because it was too old. They wanted to build a kindergarten there. I don't think anyone was opposed to a kindergarten, but it should not replace the bath as a social meeting space. I think that was an important aspect: to preserve public space for ordinary people to gather.
>
> *How did RF get involved? Were you invited to join the protests?*
> We had members living in the area. The protests were initiated by the local population, ordinary folks from the neighborhood. Then RF proposed the occupation, and the idea was supported by the locals. We ensured that we would maintain their support. No one wore masks, and we did not barricade the building. We just hung out there and organized activities. Our demand was to renovate the building instead of demolishing it.
>
> We also appointed "lifeguards." They stayed overnight. Most of the locals involved were over fifty years old. This was during winter, it was cold, there was no power. It wasn't fun to stay in the building overnight, but someone had to. Otherwise, it would have been too easy for the cops to kick us out.
>
> *Were other leftist groups involved?*
> Not that I know of.
>
> *Was the occupation important for RF?*

Yes. It was great and brought a lot of energy to the organization. Most occupations in Sweden were led by activist groups who had little contact with local residents. They built barricades and hid inside the building until it was raided by the cops. In Aspudden, we had a great relationship with the locals. They constantly brought us food, sleeping bags, and space heaters. Some just stopped by to encourage us and tell us how much they appreciated the occupation. It was a broad range of people from the neighborhood, from pensioners to small kids. We stayed for four months, which meant that the occupation lasted longer than most occupations at that time.

"A Crash Course in Political Contempt"

In 2006, the Stockholm city council had initially decided to demolish Aspuddsbadet, which had been run voluntarily for a long time. The bath was opened in 1919 in the working-class neighborhood of Aspudden. It was run by the city council until 1986. That year, the city council considered closing the bath, but the workers at the bath offered to run it on a voluntary basis. They founded a nonprofit association and came to an agreement with the city council. The nonprofit was responsible for administering and maintaining the bath; the city council's sole responsibility was the annual inspection of the building. The model proved successful until, in 2006, the nonprofit wanted to borrow money from the city. Among other things, they wanted to install a new cleaning system for the water. At the time, the city council was controlled by a center-right majority, and it decided not to loan any money to the association and to demolish the bath instead.

What followed was a long struggle to save the bath, which was held dear by many of the local residents. The protest movement founded another nonprofit, "Save Aspuddsbadet."

The protests were diverse. There were public events held in Aspudden with hot tubs, and red flags flew from the windows. The issue was also brought to court, where it went through several levels of jurisdiction. In September, the city councillor for culture and sports, Madeleine Sjöstedt from the Liberal Party, confirmed the council's decision: The bath was going to be torn down.

On September 28, Save Aspuddsbadet occupied the building. The occupation had broad support among the local population. During the first days, hundreds of people stopped by. They brought food, money, blankets, and furniture. City council clerks also showed up. The occupants asked them to leave, which they did. It was the only time that people from the city council respected the wishes of the local residents.

Save Aspuddsbadet lost one case in the courts after the other, even though the city council had great difficulties justifying their decision in any meaningful way. Minutes from city council meetings were missing. But Sjöstedt rejected any dialogue, both with the nonprofit that had run the bath for twenty years and with Save Aspuddsbadet. The only dialogue she engaged in was the one on her own blog; yet if supporters of the bath left critical comments there, they were taken down. Sjöstedt did not reply to emails either.

The occupants, who called themselves "lifeguards," were very open to discussing the issue publicly, with the politicians, the police, and the press. Each Sunday they held an open assembly in the bath, where everyone was welcome to express their opinion. Local politicians were invited as well, but the only one who ever came was Stefan Nilsson from the Green Party.

The occupants were stubborn in their defense of the bath, and public support remained high. In the immediate neighborhood, there was only a small group of property owners who stood behind the city council. All other neighbors attended the exhibitions, film screenings, and concerts that were organized in the bath's empty basin. The struggle was not just about the bath. This was a struggle against undemocratic urban planning and gentrification. It concerned not only Aspudden but many other neighborhoods in Stockholm as well. The protesters wanted to preserve a social meeting space that was essential for the local community.

"Socialism. Labor law. Antifascism. Resistance."

In the early hours of November 25, the police raided the bath and arrested the lifeguards. Neighbors who understood what was going on played loud music, and fireworks lit up the sky. It only took a few minutes for a big crowd of residents to gather and protest outside the building. Hundreds of them stayed all day while their beloved bath was emptied and boarded up.

The lifeguards continued to guard the building twenty-four hours a day to ensure that the bath wasn't going to be demolished before all legal options were exhausted. But on December 7, the once landmarked building was turned into rubble by a demolition company. The lifeguards weren't completely done yet, however. Cars and human chains prevented heavier equipment from reaching the site. The blockade lasted for three days, but on December 10, it was finally time to say goodbye to the building. At midnight, eighty people broke through the fence around the building to place roses at the entrance. The spokesperson for Save Aspuddsbadet, Ola Schubert, gave a short speech.

Save Aspuddsbadet decided to continue the fight for a social meeting space in the neighborhood and for more democratic urban planning. In early January, 160 people attended an open assembly.

The people involved in the occupation of the bath were socialists from the extraparliamentary left living in the neighborhood. It was encouraging to see that many nonpolitical residents joined the protest movement. There was a strong sense of unity and struggle.

Below follows an interview with one of the socialists involved in the occupation that originally appeared on www.revfront.org (January 29, 2010):

RF: *How did you get involved in the occupation of Aspuddsbadet?*

S: I live close by and first followed the protests in the local papers. Then I talked to a few comrades about the possibility of occupying the bath. We got in touch with the nonprofit coordinating the protests, and they had already considered the option. So we began planning. When we saw representatives of a company on site preparing for the demolition, we felt that we had to act right away. The planning wasn't really completed yet, but occupants of another building in Stockholm—the Anarchist Clinic in Liljeholmen—helped us get the water in the building hooked up, and in the evening of the very same day we had our first meeting there. Two of us stayed overnight.

RF: ***Unlike the occupants of the Anarchist Clinic, you presented yourself to the public. You were never masked and were never hiding. Why did you choose that approach?***
S: There was no reason to hide. We knew that we could only reach our goal if we were as transparent and approachable as possible. We had to make it easy for the people who wanted to support us.

RF: ***You said that you only joined the protests when the decision to demolish the bath was confirmed. Why?***
S: To be honest, because I saw it as a chance to radicalize frustrated people. The bath was great, don't get me wrong, but for me as a socialist the significance of the struggle went beyond the bath itself. The occupation radicalized hundreds of people, who supported illegal means to fight for what they believed was right. Sjöstedt and the Liberal Party had given the local residents a crash course in political contempt. From a socialist perspective, I think the protests were very successful, even if we lost the bath.

RF: ***You consider the protest a success?***
S: Absolutely! We united the neighborhood and turned it against right-wing politicians. The struggle for Aspuddsbadet was community resistance in practice.

RF: ***You had decided early on that you would not use violence to prevent eviction and the demolition of the bath. Why?***
S: We wanted to get as many people involved in the movement as possible. Violence didn't fit, even if angered locals

had all sorts of proposals, from using tire spikes against demolition trucks to throwing rocks at the police. Some of the proposals weren't all that serious, but some certainly were.

RF: ***You made it clear that everyone was welcome to protest the demolition, no matter where they stood politically. Why?***
S: Most of the people involved came from the left, but we didn't want the protest to be branded as leftist. We didn't want to allow the right-wing politicians to turn this into a question of prestige for them. In hindsight, I think that this mattered little, and that we could have politicized the occupation more.

RF: ***Now the bath is gone. I assume that's the end of the struggle.***
S: No! We are still fighting for a more democratic society, and we are many. We want an autonomous cultural center here in Aspudden, and we are planning relevant actions. We want this center to be what the bath was during the occupation! And the bath can be reerected too, at another location, either here in Aspudden or in a neighboring suburb.

RF: ***Any final words for our readers?***
S: I want to thank everyone who was involved in the occupation and who came out to support us! It was good to see the extraparliamentary left and local residents work together. During the occupation, RF members drank coffee with pensioners, and SUF members chatted with local characters. Workers, students, and youths discussed politics for days on end, with socialists right in the middle of it. The occupation proved how important noncommercial meeting spaces are for the socialist movement, and I encourage all socialists to work for such spaces.

Rinkebyhuset

Rinkebyhuset was an abandoned administration building in Rinkeby, a suburb in the northwest of Stockholm. Most neighborhoods in Rinkeby were built in the 1960s as part of the so-called

Million Program, during which modern housing facilities were to be provided to a million people in Sweden. Rinkeby is still a working-class suburb. Rinkebyhuset had been abandoned for quite some time when RF members decided, together with local residents, to occupy it, hoping to be involved in shaping the building's future. In the following interview, an RF member explains the background of the occupation:

> At the time, there were quite a few occupations in Stockholm. First in Liljeholmen, then in Aspudden. RF was very active in Aspudden and also had members in Rinkeby. The members in Rinkeby had talked to other locals about a possible occupation there. The first meeting took place in Aspuddsbadet, while it was occupied. Step by step, more people got involved. I think that, once upon a time, Rinkebyhuset was used by a local division of the city council.
>
> ***Can you describe the building?***
> It was enormous. I think it had seven stories, and it must have been a hundred meters long. We wanted to turn it into a social center, at least as long as we were able to maintain the occupation.
>
> ***How strong was the influence of RF?***
> We had members in Rinkeby. I don't think there would have been an occupation had it not been for the occupation in Aspudden. Several RF members were part of the group that first entered Rinkebyhuset, and we had members on site almost constantly. Some of them lived close by. RF was also involved in the actions and demonstrations around the building, including people from the Operative Units. But RF was not officially involved.
>
> ***Did the other occupants object to that?***
> No. No political group was officially involved. It all happened under the name "Friends of Rinkebyhuset." But everyone

Visiting the Nazi festival in Kolsva, September 2012.

who was involved knew that RF was a driving force, at least in the beginning.

What did the occupation mean for RF?
It wasn't as important as the one in Aspudden. But the Operative Units got new members! It was difficult to use the occupation for propaganda purposes, since we weren't officially involved. But I think in certain circles it changed the image that people had of RF. I think we were taken more seriously as a political group. For a long time, we were seen as little more than lefty hooligans. By the way, the axes that we used in Kolsva came from the Rinkebyhuset basement.[5]

How did the occupation end?
I don't even remember how long we were there, but it wasn't particularly long. While we were there, everything went well, the local population was on our side. But the politicians in Rinkeby could pretty much do what they wanted. Eventually, the cops simply evicted us. After that, there were only a few smaller actions.

LINKÖPING AND MORE ABOUT THE OPERATIVE UNITS

"

RF had a reputation of being much harder than AFA. When they came to Linköping, we thought they were the shit. I was sixteen years old, it wasn't much more complicated than that.

"They Were the Best at Bashing Up Nazis, and That's Exactly What We Wanted to Do"

In 2008, an RF local was formed in Linköping. It was the first RF local outside of Gothenburg and Stockholm. Two of the members had been active in AFA Linköping when they were in secondary school; two others came from a group named Linköping's Free Antifascists.

The strongest fascist organization in Linköping was NSF. Before the Swedish elections in 2006, they held several rallies as they ran candidates on the municipal level. The following interview is with a founding member of RF Linköping:

> In 2006, we were active in two different groups: AFA and Free Antifascists. When NSF held their rallies, RF members and people from the Antifascist Skinheads used to come to Linköping from Stockholm. Together, we managed to seriously mess up some of the rallies. That same year, AFA Linköping folded due to personal reasons. Two of us wanted to found RF Linköping, and two members from the Free Antifascists were eager to join.

Why did you want to be a part of RF?
Because we thought they were more badass than anyone else!

How old were you?
Sixteen. RF had a reputation of being much harder than AFA. When they came to Linköping, we thought they were the shit. I was sixteen years old, it wasn't much more complicated than that. They were the best at bashing up Nazis, and that's exactly what we wanted to do. We were politically motivated, but we didn't have much of a theoretical understanding back then. We were allowed to become prospects. After a while, we got two more people in the group, and in 2008, we all became full members and the Linköping local was officially founded.

What was expected of you as prospects?
We were able to travel to Stockholm, which was great! We went to rallies and attacked a Hallberg-Cuula commemoration at some graveyard in Solna.[1] And we fought with Nazi skins, they were still around at the time.

But in Linköping you were on your own during the trial period?
Yes, but that was not a problem. We were manic, we were teenagers!

Which fascist organizations were most active in Linköping?
NSF. For us, they were pretty old. We were sixteen, most of them were about thirty. But as I said, we were manic, we did home visits every weekend. And there were Nazi skins in Linköping too, whom we fought on the streets. We disrupted every single NSF rally.

And eventually NSF disappeared from Linköping?
Yes, you can say that. But there were a few successors, for example the Identitarian Reaction Östergötland, but we

pestered them with home visits. And there was SD, of course, we messed with them too.

You were never attacked?
Yes, we were attacked. One of us got home visits all the time, he was publicly known. It was a hectic time, but the level of violence in Linköping wasn't that high. We had fun doing what we did and didn't think much about the consequences.

Did you face repression?
At the time, hardly any. In any case, not as much as later.

It sounds as if you were a tight-knit group in Linköping. You never grew much, did you?
No. I think one more person joined later, but essentially we were always the same crew.

In 2006, the year when the youths in Linköping wanted to join RF, the organization introduced a new system. The initiative came from Stockholm. The system was built on Operative Units (OU) covering a specific geographical area. The innovative part was that people could join the Operative Units even if they weren't full RF members. You didn't even need to have any ambition to become a member; it was enough to be willing to participate in actions. Those who applied for membership first became "prospects" and went through a trial period, which could take up to two years, as in the case of the Linköping youths.

To belong to an Operative Unit meant that you were not obliged to participate in any RF activities. But you didn't have a right to participate in any activities of your choosing either. There were regular meetings, in which both RF members and OU associates came together. The meetings were usually held in conjunction with bigger events such as the Salem March or the Swedish National Day.[2] Social activities and educational programs were organized on those occasions as well.

The OU system allowed RF to mobilize a big number of

people when needed, but it also made both the antifascist and the political work easier on an everyday level. In 2007, Stockholm had Operative Units in the west, north, and south of the city. In the south, they were divided along the subway and commuter train lines. The units had fancy names such as "The Northern Division," "The Southern Commando of the Capital," and "Commando Assata Shakur." In Gothenburg, they carried simpler names such as "Operative Unit Northeast" or "Operative Unit Hammarkullen" (a Gothenburg suburb).

The level of activity varied from unit to unit. It depended on how big the unit was and how much time the associates had for political activities. It was not expected that OU associates would dedicate the same amount of time to political work as RF members did. RF members had to meet high expectations. They were expected to be disciplined and to dedicate a lot of time to the organization. Their participation in meetings and actions was obligatory.

The OU system was never used in Linköping and Örebro, because the towns and the locals were too small. But in these towns, there were "free agents" who supported the locals without obligations.

In Gothenburg, the OU system was used until RF folded. In Stockholm, it essentially disappeared in 2010 after many members had left, making the local much smaller than in previous years.

MEMORY "THEY CAN LIE AS MUCH AS THEY WANT: EVERYONE KNOWS THAT RF NEVER EVADES A FIGHT, NO MATTER THE NUMBERS."

"Some of our members were standing trial. We hadn't been sure if we'd be able to travel to Västerås, since the trial was on a weekday, I was supposed to work, and we didn't know whether we could find a car and a driver. But the night before, we got everything organized, and the next morning, five of us were traveling to Västerås: four comrades from RF and one from AFA.

The driver had not been an RF member for long, but he had been with us during several actions, so I knew that I could rely on him as much as on the others. Even though there were only five of us, we drove to Västerås feeling that we could take on the entire Nazi scene. We had brand-new safety vests with us, which made us feel even more invincible. I was also carrying a small axe that a comrade had brought with him from abroad. In other cases, this would have felt exaggerated, but since we were so few and didn't know what to expect, I figured it couldn't hurt.

We heard in the car that the comrades from Linköping were on their way too. I don't recall if they were still prospects at the time or already full members, but I had met them before. We were also expecting comrades of the accused from Örebro and the local comrades from Västerås. The latter were not RF members, and so we didn't know how they would fare during an action. Such were the circumstances as we rode into town.

We parked the car at the railway station and went to the center. We had agreed on meeting our comrades at another car, on the other side of town. As we were crossing a park, we ran into a group of Nazis. They were young, maybe eighteen, and gone as soon as one of us poured his tea over their heads. More wasn't needed. We were hoping that these prodigies were summoning more experienced Nazis to the park, but no one came. Maybe they had already gathered downtown?

We continued and reached the city library, where we waited for the comrades from Linköping. When they arrived, we heard that the comrades who would later form RF Örebro were already at the courthouse—together with a group of Nazis. I started feeling the adrenaline. Now we were eight.

As we're leaving the library, a police patrol car drives past us. I decide to ditch the axe. It was a shame to lose it, but a necessary precaution, since the cops were already observing us. We're heading to the courthouse, which, again, is on the other side of town, beyond the train tracks and the railway station. On the way, we hear that there have already been confrontations at the courthouse and that the Nazis have been thrown out. We assume that they are heading our way. We send the newbie and one of the women in our group ahead as scouts. The rest of us wait in a park next to the railway station.

After a while, we get a call from the scouts. About eighteen Nazis are approaching us. We are only six, since we lost the scouts. And even when they make it back, we are only half of what the Nazis are. We look for things we can use as weapons, but the park doesn't provide us with much. We understand that this might get tricky, and I regret having ditched the axe.

We are still looking for possible weapons when we notice a group of men exiting the railway station. That must be them! I tell everyone that the shit is about to hit the fan, and that it is best for us to take the initiative. So we go through the park right toward them. They have not yet noticed us, but soon we'll have to leave the park and cross a road. At that point, they won't be able to miss us.

We get to the pedestrian crossing and are maybe fifty yards away. Now they see us! "Let's go!" I yell and start running without waiting for a reaction from my comrades. I know that the comrades from Stockholm will deliver. As soon as I step onto the road, all anxiety is gone. I see that all of us are running with me, the comrades from Jönköping included. Everyone wants to get to the Nazis first. In RF, it was always a badge of honor to get the first punch in and open the fight.

As soon as the Nazis see us running toward them, they run away. Their ugly smirks are gone. They might have felt superior when they first saw us, but not now. We attack despite being outnumbered, which means that we've already won. They can lie as much as they want: Everyone knows that RF never evades a fight, no matter the numbers.

By the time we've made it across the road, the Nazis have retreated into the railway station, where they grab bottles from a store. As we head to the store, the bottles come flying and we can't get in. Our only weapon is a bag of dog shit one of us found in the park. It lands right in the face of one of the fascists. I run to a café around the corner to get something for us to throw. When I return, the scouts have arrived. But there's a security guard who also wants to get involved. With him and his baton behind us, and still no chance to get into the store, we choose a different approach and split into two groups. My group heads for a nearby shopping mall, where we take the elevator to the top floor. There, we find a couple of pallets, which we intend to throw on the Nazis when they appear—but they never do. The other group has gone to a different shopping mall, where they brawl with a smaller group of Nazis, who they leave behind bloodied. The second victory of the day! We decide to leave our shopping mall and head back to the library to reunite with the others and maybe meet some more antifas.

On the way, we are stopped by cops and searched. We have no weapons on us, but some of us are wearing safety vests. The police run a search in their register, and seconds later we are led to one of their vans. They lock us in different cells. We have to wait. In the best case, they'll let us go without a citation; in the worst, they'll keep us for a while.

A few hours later, they let us go. It's dark outside. At first, I don't see anything, but then I recognize several comrades who are there to greet us. My friends from Stockholm are among them. We say goodbye to the comrades from Västerås and Linköping and are escorted to the highway by two police cars. On the way home, I learn that we scored a few more wins in Västerås that day. We are in a good mood and happy about having been able to strengthen our connections to RF comrades from other locals.

—Written by a former RF Stockholm member

2009–2014

ÖREBRO AND MORE ABOUT HOME VISITS

"

Our actions became quite intense, and the media began to report about them. And when the media reports about things, the politicians have to react. I believe a big factor was that 2014 was an election year, when it became important to tackle "political extremism."

"It's Easier to Commit Violent Crime in the Countryside"

RF kept on growing. In 2009, a local was formed in Örebro. The majority of the local's members were former members of AFA Örebro, but they had dissolved the AFA local to found the RF local. The group was small, but it remained active until RF dissolved in 2015.

RF Örebro had a few special characteristics. For example, its members weren't allowed to consume drugs, even privately. Any member who consumed drugs was suspended. The arguments were, first, that all members represented RF Örebro at any given time and, second, that drug consumption had detrimental social consequences. RF Örebro was the RF local that took the clearest stance against alcohol and drug consumption.

In 2012, a few teenagers from Eskilstuna sought membership in RF. They, too, were from the hardcore punk scene, straight edge, and vegan. They had been fighting fascists in their hometown for several years, for a while in AFA's name. They were integrated into RF Örebro.

Below are two interviews with RF Örebro members.

"We Didn't Do Much More than Antifascism, That Kept Us Busy Enough"

How did you become an RF member?
I wanted to join AFA Örebro, but then all of the AFA members went to RF. I had been traveling to demonstrations in Stockholm since I was fifteen, but I only got interested in getting organized when I was eighteen. And under the circumstances, RF was the best option. I hadn't even heard of RF when I sought membership in AFA.

But you were okay with everyone moving from AFA to RF?
Yes. For half a year, I was a prospect, then I became a full member. That was in 2010, I believe. We were officially RF Örebro, but the most active members came from Köping and Eskilstuna.

How many were you?
Six full members, I believe. With hangarounds, we were probably twelve. We never actively looked for new members. We always remained a pretty tight-knit group.

What was your focus?
Antifascism. There were active Nazis in Hallstahammar, Surahammar, Köping, Västerås, and other towns. We didn't do much more than antifascism, that kept us busy enough. Our goal was to prevent the Nazis from building their structures.

Apparently, your local had a few special characteristics.
Yes, drugs were frowned upon, and not just during actions but in general. We felt that we always had to represent our group in the best possible way. Everyone had to be active too, and attend the meetings. But that applied to other locals as well.

At times, we were criticized by other RF members because our antifascist work had a very strong personal dimension and we were doing so many actions. We didn't think much about security at the time. I think the critique mainly came from Stockholm.

Would you agree with it from today's perspective?
No. We were dealing with Nazis. And too many actions? I think that was positive, not negative.

In many ways, RF Örebro represented the second generation of RF: disciplined, uncompromising, very active, very militant, taking great risks. Less street fighting, more home visits. A home visit originally meant going to the home of a fascist and spray-painting messages on their walls or across their windows. But RF then took this a step further. RF Örebro also broke into the homes of fascists, smashed furniture, and took computers with them.

RF Örebro covered a big geographical area. The RF spirit was strong in Örebro. But the group was adapting to new circumstances as well. While Nazis had been a common sight in Örebro in the early 2000s, they had all but disappeared from the streets when RF Örebro was founded, not least because of the antifascist resistance. This, however, didn't mean that they had disappeared entirely; they had just moved elsewhere. RF Örebro had quite an impact on political developments in the region.

"RF Kicks Ass, We Ought to Join Them!"

When did you join RF?
That was in 2012, and I stayed until RF dissolved. Originally, we wanted to join RF Stockholm because Eskilstuna is fairly close.

Had you and your friends in Eskilstuna been active before?
Yes, we did our own thing, but eventually we said, "RF kicks ass, we ought to join them!" So we sought membership in Stockholm, but they sent us to Örebro. I'm not sure why. Maybe it seemed like a better fit. We also knew RF members in Örebro from earlier actions. Even if the name

"Nazi scum!" Örebro, 2009.

was RF Örebro, we covered a much wider area, the entire Mälaren Valley.

So you continued to work with the same people, but now under the name of RF?

Yes. RF was known for its militancy, and it had a structure. We thought that we'd be able to do bigger and better things within that framework. The name added weight to our actions, and the organization helped us get certain resources.

Can you say a little more about your previous experiences in antifa work?

We attacked Nazis long before we became RF. Our actions weren't always very well thought through, but we didn't have anything to prove when we joined RF. They knew what kind of people we were and what we were able to do.

The biggest difference after joining RF was that we could work more systematically. Before we joined RF, our primary targets were skinheads wearing Nazi symbols. Now we could turn to organized Nazis with the help of proper research. We had already moved in that direction before we became RF members. We were no longer just heading into town, hitting the first Nazi we saw. Instead we tried to figure out where and when they met, and so on. Our actions became less random.

You became well known for your home visits, and not only within the autonomous left—there was a lot of coverage in mainstream media. But I've heard that you were criticized for the home visits within RF as well. Is that true?
What?! No, I don't recall any of that. Okay, seriously: Yes, I think there was criticism, or at least discussion. But honestly, we didn't care much.

I'm under the impression that, for a while, you were the most active RF local. Is that right?
Yes. We were young and highly motivated. That might have been one reason. But I think that it was just easier to be active in the countryside. It's easier to commit violent crime there, there's less surveillance. At least that's how it was when we started. Soon, there was plenty of surveillance.

How strong was the repression?
It changed. In the beginning, we felt that the cops didn't give a flying fuck about us and that we could do whatever we wanted. No one seemed to care.

Why did that change, do you think?
Our actions became quite intense, and the media began to report about them. And when the media reports about things, the politicians have to react. I believe a big factor was that 2014 was an election year, when it became important to tackle "political extremism." But I'm not sure.

For many years, RF was opposed to home visits. One reason was that the organization's focus was on the streets. Another was

Örebro, November 9, 2010.

that home visits were seen as cowardly. But this changed after the fascists had retreated from the public sphere. No local did as many home visits as RF Örebro. They went to places in the entire Mälaren Valley and filmed almost all of their visits with a GoPro camera. The material was then used for RF propaganda.

MEMORY DRAKENSKÖLDSGATAN[1]

"I wake up because of glass shattering. I know right away what that means: The Nazis are here. Not hesitating for a second, I grab a knife and jump out the window where the noise is coming from. All I'm wearing are my underpants. I land on the street close to six masked Nazis with clubs and baseball bats. They have smashed the glass of the entrance to the apartment building I'm sleeping in. They seem surprised when I attack them right away, yelling obscenities and "RF!" My blood is boiling, I am mad, and I almost cut one of them with my knife. Confused, they disperse for a moment. Then they start their counterattack. One by one, they dare come at me. Even though I can avoid most of the swings of their clubs and bats, I suffer a few heavy blows and start retreating toward a bridge nearby. I move along a wall so they can't circle me. One of them takes a swing at my head with a telescopic baton (I think that's what it was), but I block the baton with one arm and stab him with the other. I pierce his lung while yelling at him. He staggers.

Now I see a comrade of mine, who was sleeping in the same apartment, jump through the same window I did. He isn't wearing more than his underpants either, but he carries two knives, one in each hand. That's too much for the Nazis, and they bail. Seconds later, I see blue lights flashing and a patrol car speeding around the corner. There is no point in trying to escape; my comrade and I are caught in the middle of the bridge. The cops arrest us. The Nazis got away at the very last second. All in all, the fight might have lasted a minute, not more.

All things considered, I pulled through all right. The biggest damage I caused myself, by jumping out the window. I tore tissue in my heel and had to use crutches for a month. Later, I was prosecuted for attempted murder and spent a month in jail before being acquitted. Neither my friend nor the Nazis went to trial.

—Written by a former RF Örebro member

DIRECTION: CHANGE

"

In Gothenburg, there was a generational shift around 2009. The football hooligans were more or less gone, and the Nazis on the streets as well. There was a shift in Stockholm too. For example, the Little League disappeared. My impression was that the changes caused fewer problems in Gothenburg than they did in Stockholm.

"Most of Them Liked to Fight"

Even if, in the late 2000s, Nazis were no longer as present on the streets of Sweden as before, they were still there. ND split, with one faction returning to SD. NSF dissolved in 2008, with the Party of the Swedes (PoS) serving as a successor.[1] PoS intended to follow in the footsteps of SD and present itself as a serious party focusing on the parliamentary path. It was unsuccessful and folded in 2015.

The parliamentary turn of the far right did, of course, impact RF. The organization had to adapt to new conditions, and it wasn't easy. For years, fighting Nazis on the streets had been at the center of RF's activism. Its identity was strongly tied to its militancy.

From the outside, the changes in the organization might not have been that obvious. But internally, RF had to deal with the fact that some new members lacked street-fighting experience. The code "Whenever, wherever, and in whatever way" could no longer serve as a general directive. Physical confrontations had to be prepared for differently; it was important to have the upper hand, and numbers became more of an issue.

In 2009 and 2010, there was a generational shift within RF, both in Gothenburg and in Stockholm. Some of the older members left the organization. The reasons were often personal. Some members who had been in RF for years wanted to do other things. Especially in Stockholm, most of the original members were gone, and most remaining members had been in the organization for only a relatively short time.

One consequence of the generational shift was that the ideological divides shifted too, and largely lost significance. In Stockholm, the anarchist influence of the founding years had practically been lost, and the ideological outlook had become more diffuse. As a consequence, RF finally introduced a central committee in 2012, agreed upon at a nationwide meeting. RF Stockholm had long been opposed to the idea.

On the following pages, we'll hear from members who remained active in RF after the generational shift and from members who joined thereafter.

"We Sat There and Talked About Marx and Such"

How was it to be active in RF Gothenburg in 2011? The group was quite big, right?

It was fun. I have always been a bit of a fetishist when it comes to political organizing, so it was cool to be active in a well-structured and functioning group. Some of us may have been too fetishist about political organizing, but we had good dynamics.

And several working groups ...

Yes, we had working groups for class struggle, antifascism, and—what was the last one again?—yes, social events! That one was, essentially, the fundraising group.

In which group were you?

Class struggle.

What did you do?
We organized reading circles, but they weren't very popular, ha ha! We also were responsible for public campaigns, we got involved in workplace conflicts, and so on. Propaganda, that was also our responsibility!

Why were the reading circles not so popular?
People were tired, didn't have enough energy. And then we sat there and talked about Marx and such ...

Were the reading circles obligatory?
Sometimes. But then everybody hated us ...

What was the relationship like with the rest of the left?
Personally, I had no contact with AFA, but others did. I never liked AFA. I think it started with not agreeing with how their research group handled things.

What do you mean?
For example, they knew about an informant in our movement but didn't tell us. Then, one time, they wanted an SMR defector to join us during an anti-National Day event, even though he had bashed up his girlfriend really bad.[2] Their argument was that the Nazis needed to know that we knew about the guy's history, or something like that—I never really got it. In any case, guys who beat up their girlfriends have no place at our events.

Were you close to other RF locals?
Yes, at least to Örebro. We didn't have too much contact with Stockholm, they had internal problems all the time. In Gothenburg, there was a generational shift around 2009. The football hooligans were more or less gone, and the Nazis on the streets as well. There was a shift in Stockholm too. For example, the Little League disappeared. My impression was that the changes caused fewer problems in Gothenburg than they did in Stockholm.

Was RF still proud not to be like the rest of the autonomous left?
The jargon in RF was still different. I think that was important. When we talked about class politics, it was rooted in reality. That was a big difference from other groups on the left, even if all were socialists. But the language wasn't crucial in attracting people who didn't care much for political organizing otherwise. I think the way we looked and carried ourselves was more important.

NO PEACE FOR TEMP AGENCIES!

The following originally appeared on www.revfront.org (April 18, 2011):

In the spring, RF will run a campaign against temp agencies.

Temp agencies were illegal in Sweden before the center-right government of the early 1990s made them legal. Since then, they have become an ever-increasing problem for the working class. Insecure employment has become the norm because of them. In addition, they are used to circumnavigate labor laws protecting workers. They undermine solidarity at the workplace and divide workers into different categories: workers with "proper," long-term contracts and workers with temporary contracts. Temp workers can't get organized in unions and are moved from workplace to workplace. Temp agencies exploit primarily the youngest, least educated, and most precarious sections of the working class. We, the workers who can't get any other jobs, must accept what they offer us.

Temp agencies have stood in the way of creating a better life for working-class people for two decades now. Those who have studied history know that workplace organizing and daily struggles with the bosses are crucial for our survival as a class, regardless of our ethnicity, age, or political orientation. Organizing your workplace is the strongest weapon in the class struggle. Insecure employment creates insecure lives. Many of us have experiences with temp agencies. We've

"1931–2011: 90 years since Ådalen. Against strikebreaking and starvation wages. Keep temp agencies prohibited!" Gothenburg, May 1, 2011.

been treated like shit, have worked under dismal conditions, and have not received our wages. And if we speak up, we are threatened with no longer getting any jobs at all.

We want to hear your stories! Tell us about your experiences with temp agencies and insecure employment. Everything helps our campaign! You can, of course, remain anonymous.

"If You Had Done Your Years on the Streets, It Was Okay Wanting to Do Something Else"

What's your story? How did you come to RF, and why did you want to be a member?

Before I joined RF, I wasn't particularly active. Then, one day, I just sent RF an email. About a year earlier, I had sent an email to AFA but never received a response. That email might not have been very clear, because AFA's membership criteria weren't very clear. On the one hand, they had this open network-type structure, but on the other hand, they were quite closed. They had slogans such as "You're not a member of AFA, you are AFA!" Sounded like an identity crisis to me.

I discovered RF through AFA, because both groups collaborated in 2009 during the War Against the Free Nationalists. They referenced each other in their statements, as no group was allowed to claim an action for itself. There were other antifa groups around as well, and it was correct to acknowledge all of them.

So when you joined RF, the relationship with AFA was fine?
No, it wasn't, but I can only speak for Gothenburg. I became a member right after the War Against the Free Nationalists. The Free Nationalists' network was in tatters, but GFN was still around. So RF still went looking for them, when there were far-right demonstrations and such. At the time, there was a lot of bitterness between RF and AFA because of a few incidents. There was a story about a video that one group had apparently stolen from the other, I don't know. But more important was the thing with the money. AFA had quite a big network and they did many fundraisers, which meant that they had quite a lot of money, but RF felt that AFA wasn't doing anything meaningful with it. And, I mean, it's true, AFA Gothenburg wasn't particularly active when I joined RF. So RF wanted to get the money, since RF was much more active, but AFA said that it was their money and gave it to SUF.

Did you see AFA as a militant antifascist group?
Yes, they were militant, but there was a tradition in RF Gothenburg of badmouthing AFA. It was started by the generation before me. People made fun of the "nerds" who joined AFA and all of that. I did the same, but I have to say, every time I looked at AFA more closely, I found that image confirmed. Sure, you can look at things through a lens that won't allow any other conclusions, but here are a few examples: Once, there was a rally in solidarity with a mosque in

Gothenburg that had been attacked by Nazis, and while we went around and bashed up GFN members, AFA was at the demo with a banner. Sure, banners have their place, but for me, that was just pathetic. I had similar experiences with other AFA locals. Once, we drove to Skåne to help a new leftist group get off the ground.[3] We gave a presentation and did security for an event they had organized. We arrived a little late, and SMR was already there, and the first thing we did was fight them. We weren't prepared and had no masks, but what else should we have done? SMR was right outside the venue, and we needed to get them away. And what did AFA do? They threw bottles from a safe distance.

Often, I didn't even know who AFA was. In my world, everyone who was not RF was AFA. Of course, that wasn't true. Anyway, I still carry an image from that day in Skåne with me: One of our prospects was so mad that he went to a masked dude in a North Face jacket and yelled right in his face: "Hey, why are you just standing there without doing anything?!"

How did the tensions between RF and AFA affect RF's work?
Positively as well as negatively, I think. When I became a member, RF didn't do any home visits, for example. Whenever someone raised the idea, people laughed and said, "That's AFA stuff, we don't do that!" End of discussion.

Sometimes it can be a good thing to make different positions clear, but in this case it led to problems that cost plenty of time. Collaboration always sounds good, but there is no denying that we thrived on the reputation of being harder than AFA. That's why people came to us, especially the people we wanted to come to us. AFA almost entirely stopped claiming actions, while we did the exact opposite, which helped our reputation.

If you looked at the far right's online forums, they often wrote that AFA was dead, but they always sent out warnings about RF! This helped us and not AFA. It mainly had to do with our practice, of course, not with our political beliefs. Those weren't too different from AFA's.

Back to you seeking membership in RF. How did that play out?
It was a very serious process. Perhaps it got more relaxed later on, or perhaps they did things very thoroughly in my case because they didn't know me and I didn't know much about the inner structure of RF. In any case, I had to meet two members in a public space in Gothenburg, I had to show my ID, and then we went to a bar (no alcohol!), where they asked me a ton of questions. Many were about politics, they wanted to know my opinion on various issues and why I held those opinions. I was very impressed by it all. It was a little like seeking membership in a hooligan firm.

And your goal was to become a full member, not just an OU associate?
Yes. I started as a prospect.

How long did it take before you became a full member?
Eight months perhaps? I had a patron during that time, with whom I had much contact. I think I was lucky to join RF when there was new energy, a new fire. 2010 was also an election year, people are always politicized during an election year.

What was the fascist scene like in Gothenburg at the time?
GFN was still around, and there was the Nordic Youth, but they split into a Christian faction, kinda like a sect, and an activist wing, *querfront* types.[4] The latter was stronger in Gothenburg. ND was still around too, they had always been quite strong on the west coast.

Were these groups active on the streets?
GFN to some degree. But they no longer were a real threat. The Nordic Youth never was a threat. If they did an action, it was directed at schoolteachers, the immigration office, things

like that. For the left and us, they posed no danger. They were mainly students. Okay, there are tough students too, but they were of the weaker kind.

There were no more physical confrontations on the streets?
There were some. We were still looking for some, since it was such an important part of our history. But times had changed. Once, GFN showed up to an SD event downtown with a banner. Had that happened a few years earlier, there would have been chaos right away. But now there were too many cops, and we couldn't get to them. A couple of things were thrown, I believe, we taunted them, but that was it. It wasn't that the will was missing, it's just that repression had become too strong. Besides, for a real brawl, there needs to be will from both sides, but GFN was really weak at that point, they had lost many members, gone through a split—they weren't as well prepared for confrontations as they had been earlier. The football thing was important too. GFN had recruited quite a bit from the Wisemen, IFK's hooligan firm. But eventually the Wisemen leaders lost patience with it and gave the Nazis an ultimatum: "Boys, you gotta chose. Either you are hooligans or Nazis, you can't be both." And most of them stayed with the Wisemen. A Communist Party member was offered the same choice, and he chose the party. In any case, GFN had lost many of its best street fighters, and one of their leading figures had defected to the left.

I think one reason why many of the hools stuck to football was that fighting there was different. You bandaged your hands and wore mouthguards, that was it. You weren't supposed to bring even brass knuckles. The political fights were dirtier, and that wasn't their thing.

Can you tell us more about RF's class politics?
RF started to do more home visits in 2011, since the Nazis had disappeared from the streets. There was no Nazi organization in Gothenburg that was really strong. When one appeared,

"No robberies, no burglaries, no drug trade. This is a working-class neighborhood. Don't hurt your own people!"

it was usually gone after six months. So we were looking for things to do apart from antifascism, and by coincidence we were drawn into a workplace struggle. That was great! Finally, we could take on a role that we had always wanted to have—namely, to be a resource for the resistance of the class. We did the groundwork for workplace struggles. When the workers planned a protest, we mobilized, put up posters, made banners. This allowed them to take on the bosses in the factory. In 2010, we ran a housing campaign, which was well received. The more such things we did, the more the membership changed, of course. Now there were people who wanted to join RF without militant antifascism being their number one interest. For a while, we had people who didn't do antifascist work at all. This created tensions, because the political practice of the members was now very different.

Some didn't participate in militant antifascism?

That's right. And in general there was no problem with that. Okay, that's only partly true. There was no problem with it, but there still was. I guess you can put it this way: If you had done your years on the streets, it was okay wanting to do something else, but not otherwise.

I understand you had different working groups.
Correct. I was in the one for antifascism. We were a group of comrades who were very tight and did plenty of things together privately as well. It was one of the reasons why we were very effective. The disadvantage was that it led to an imbalance of power within the organization, an informal hierarchy. When we had meetings, the working groups could end up competing with one another. Sounds silly, but that's how it was. Our group was accused of being elitist or of withholding information. It was complicated. Since we were so tight, also privately, we had many informal discussions. And it's true, we should have had some of those discussions at the meetings instead.

How would you characterize RF ideologically at the time? Was it still diverse?
Yes, and I think that was a strength, although it wasn't as rosy as some make it out to be. We liked the reputation of attracting people to political work who wouldn't do any otherwise, but where are those people today? Why are they no longer active? Did they really get a proper political education in RF?

How do you remember the relationship between the different locals?
When I became a member, it was good. But there was always an ideological tension. With regard to Stockholm, we always felt that they were "doing their thing," but that didn't have so much to do with ideology. We had very good contacts to Örebro and Linköping. We actually didn't know that much about Stockholm. For a long time, all contact with Stockholm had gone through one person, and that person had left the organization. After that, it almost felt that we had more

contact with AFA Stockholm than with RF Stockholm—at least with two AFA members.

How about repression?

It became worse after the Kinnunen incident of 2009.[5] After that, SÄPO kept a much closer eye on us, and it became near impossible to target SD. When SD entered parliament in 2010, everything changed. During the election campaign, we were still able to burn flares at their rallies without the cops interfering. Four years later, we couldn't even get close enough to throw anything at their rallies.

The increased repression had several reasons: SD was in parliament, the police were much better equipped technologically, and the left was under general scrutiny. The cops knew much more about us than before. One of the RF founders liked to share the first statement he ever heard a cop make about RF: "I get AFA, they are political. But RF, they are just criminals!" The cops didn't understand what RF was. "They don't look like lefties, and they steal shit from Nazis, so ... they must be criminals!"

How did RF respond to the repression? What effect did it have on your political work?

These questions are hard to answer, at least for me. I have changed since I was in RF and gained some distance. At the time, I was a fanatic. For example, I thought we did too much prisoner solidarity work. My thoughts were: "Okay, we are all aware of the risks. Sure, it's not fun to be sentenced to prison, but that's a risk we take, so get on with it." Of course, I was for writing letters and for sending money to prisoners. But with all the money we raised for them, we could have done plenty of political work! For example, we didn't have our own car, so we always had to borrow AFA's. And then, one time, we crashed their car, and after that we were no longer allowed to borrow it. Instead, we had yet another conflict with AFA. But in hindsight, I understand the importance of prisoner solidarity work, and I might just not have been a very good comrade back then. It's a feeling I have quite often when I think about my time in RF: I guess I was too dogmatic and a bit of a tyrant.

What's your view on RF's propaganda? I'm also thinking about how violence was portrayed.

People like black-and-white answers to questions like these. I have discussed this many times, because I was a big supporter of the propaganda we did. I don't want to exaggerate my role, but I was very active in RF, dedicated a lot of my time to the organization, and I was always pushing for more militancy and for documenting every single bit of it. When others thought we should lie low for a little while, I thought we should double down. For example, I never liked to talk about "confrontations" with Nazis. I thought that was rhetorical whitewashing. I wanted us to call things by their name: We didn't have "confrontations" with Nazis, we fucked them up. The harder the rhetoric, the better for me. I wanted RF to be seen as a monster, kinda like a golem in Jewish culture—a monster that can be used for good things but that doesn't have to be good as such. You can laugh about it, but that was my approach. Sophisticated wording and clever arguments were for others. RF had one purpose only: to be as nasty as possible and to strike as much fear into Nazis as possible.

Didn't that create conflicts within the Gothenburg local when you had members who weren't involved in militant antifascism at all?

Sometimes. I guess I was longing for the good old days, but I also understood that RF had to change. There was hard rhetoric in 1917 or in the 1930s too, but that didn't stop people from doing political work as well. If we set the agenda, both are possible.

But let me get back to your question about propaganda. As I said, people like black-and-white answers to such questions, they want to hear that something was either entirely good or entirely bad. But I think it's impossible to give such answers, because it always depends on your personal perspective. I always followed the motto "High risk, high reward." I was schooled that way. When I joined RF, it was clear to me that "We do what we do until we get caught." That was the plan, and you wouldn't stop before it happened. And this is where the propaganda videos come into play: They served as a deterrent, so there was high reward. The Nazis could claim on their online forums that AFA no longer existed, because even if it wasn't true, it was hard to prove that, because AFA never claimed any actions. With RF, it was the complete opposite. Take the Backaplan action of 2012, when GFN members got a beating and left their leader behind.[6] They wrote online that they—glorious patriots!—had defended women and children despite being outnumbered. All lies. And then we uploaded a video that showed the truth: no women, no children, only a bunch of Nazis abandoning their leader, who gets beaten to a pulp. There was no arguing with that video.

On the downside, the videos made repression much worse. *Uppdrag Granskning* made a big deal of them in their program about us.[7] They say that the police are here to fight crime, but it is not coincidental that they stand for "law and order." Their main duty is to defend the system, which makes it paramount to lock up folks who do not look like criminals but who commit, document, and brag about criminal acts. That's more important than locking up people who do crime in secret.

The propaganda was a risk, but I thought it was a risk worth taking. That was an important difference between RF and AFA: We took higher risks and got more shit done. Both things are directly related. I am still convinced of that, but today I can wonder about whether it was worth the personal price that many paid. But, well, in RF Gothenburg we quoted Russian nihilists rather than Karl Marx. "The revolutionary is a doomed man!" That's what we believed in. People like us couldn't expect a happy life.

RF's membership changed as the organization grew bigger and the Nazis disappeared from the streets. Even for some new members, the RF they became part of wasn't what they had thought it was. Militancy was no longer as central, and there were tensions between the local groups. The "RF spirit," however, was still held high.

"When I Became a Member, We Cherished That Reputation and Did Everything to Keep It Up"

How did you come to RF?
I had been politically active before, but I never felt that I fit into the leftist scene very well. Something was always wrong with me. In RF, I felt at home. It was much less pretentious.

What kind of people were drawn to RF? Did the organization reach out to specific groups?
Many who joined already had personal contacts with RF members. Others came from the autonomous left, and some came from God knows where. RF recruited primarily within the working class, but I don't think that it was the class background that made RF stand out within the left. I think it was more the attitude and certain positions. At least that's how it was when I joined. Most AFA members were nerds in our eyes—maybe not in Stockholm, where there were two solid AFA members who spent a lot of time with RF and were more RF than most in AFA.

Many say that it was important for RF to be different from other leftist groups.
Absolutely, that was very important. We weren't interested in the subculture that was so important for them. We wanted to be open to ordinary folks. It was similar to what the Communist Party of Sweden always claimed: "We are not part of the left movement, we are our own movement!" Of course, we attracted a special kind of people. I would

"The crisis is their fault. Sink the right!" Stockholm, September 2009.

have never dived into politics that much had it not been for RF. And that was true for many others. I think it's the reason why so few of them are active now. RF offered a very special framework for political work. There is no equivalent to that today. And RF never got much credit within the left. There were a lot of negative connotations—the machismo, the drugs. But even RF's worst critics within the left have to admit that RF were the only ones who could protect the rest of the left from the Nazis. We had a reputation of being crazy, and other leftist groups feared and respected us at the same time. When I became a member, we cherished that reputation and did everything to keep it up.

Did the other leftist groups also perceive you as different?
Oh yes. Some didn't want to have anything to do with RF. I was involved in Action Against Deportation, and people there were very surprised that I was in RF.[8] RF confused many people. "They aren't left—or, okay, they are in a way." The relationship was similar to the one between the Moderate Party and SD: On the one hand, the Moderates roll their eyes whenever SD is mentioned, but on the other hand, they know

that they need SD.[9] I think the rest of the left never really knew how to relate to us. The debates about machismo and toxic masculinity were never-ending.

CHILDREN: CLASS SOCIETY'S BIGGEST LOSERS

The following originally appeared on www.revfront.org (February 4, 2011):

Swedish politicians have long stopped talking about class. Today, there is no radical working-class alternative in parliament. The working class has no representatives in the corridors of power. But those not brainwashed by bourgeois media and populist sloganeering see society as it is: divided. We know who the biggest winners are. But who are the biggest losers? They are the weakest in society, who, at the same time, society's future rests on. In Sweden, about 220,000 children live in families that do not have enough money for the most essential things: food, clothes, a roof over their head. This number has increased in recent years and will continue to increase. According to a report by Save the Children Sweden, the number of children living in poverty rose from 10.9 to 11.5 percent during the year 2009 alone. Most affected are children of single parents whose average income has decreased by 5 percent. While middle-class kids waltz around in expensive designer clothes and douse each other in champagne, we, the children of the working class, are forced to sell our labor for slave wages in order to survive. In primary and secondary school, meals are still free, but that's not the case in all high schools.[10] Municipalities have discovered the meals as a source of income and let students pay for them. They say what they charge is modest and would affect neither the students' eating habits nor the family's budget—oh, and yes, they fill in the detail that the municipality also needs the money. But the income generated by school meals is negligible for the municipality, while the costs can be significant for struggling families. For many

children, the meal at school is the only nutritious meal all day. We demand that free meals in all schools, public and private, are stipulated by law![11]

"It Was Expected from Members That They Were Willing and Able to Engage in Violence"

How ideological was RF?
It was always important to be open to ordinary people. You weren't required to have read Lenin—or anything, for that matter—to come to RF. On the other hand, it was also important that RF was not just about beating up Nazis but that there were political reasons for it. Did we offer much in terms of political education? I don't think so. Or I forgot. I remember us encouraging members to educate themselves and to understand why fascism was a threat to the working class. Personally, I didn't focus on class politics, but it was part of RF.

Did all members have to engage in violence?
Yes, you can say that. It was expected from members that they were willing and able to engage in violence. But no one could become a member who had no politics at all. You had to be able to explain why you wanted to be an RF member. If RF considered you suitable, you became a prospect. As a prospect, you didn't necessarily have to prove yourself by doing illegal things, but you had to work with the members, help with propaganda, maybe do some scouting, things like that.

A lot has been said about RF being different than the rest of the autonomous left. What was your impression? And what was the meaning of terms such as "RF material" and "RF spirit"?
I think that RF demanded more from its members than other groups. You couldn't just do whatever you wanted in the name of RF. In AFA, that was possible. AFA Stockholm, for example, just did their own thing. In RF, you couldn't do that.

RF was RF, no matter where. In that sense, RF was more centralist. There were common expectations about what members had to do and how they presented themselves. It was good if you were tough and didn't get nervous too easily.

Did the membership live up to these expectations?
I think so. People always have their own characteristics, but everyone in RF was reliable. Okay, some might have been less stable than others, having a bit of a temper and such. But for people who didn't have their shit together at all, there was no place in RF. You could always trust an RF comrade.

Was discipline higher than in other groups?
Again, I think that was true. I was never in another organization, but I have moved in leftist circles long enough to know that there were significant differences.

How did you experience the relationship between RF and the rest of the left?
We made many jokes about how shitty all the others were! But that was just part of the jargon, it wasn't true. Of course there were good people in other groups as well, but there was always some competition about who was best and hardest. We celebrated that. Not a big problem for me. We embraced the image of RF being "the furthest to the left" and "the most badass" in order to influence the political climate and to create a bit of breathing room for other leftist groups, since they could always say, "Hey, there are people much worse than we are!" In addition, we were responsible for the entire left's security. We made sure that leftist events weren't attacked. The Nazis knew that they'd have it coming if they tried.

In 2012, a motion was passed at a nationwide RF meeting that had been rejected numerous times before: the installment of a central committee. The anarchist wing within the organization remained critical of the decision. Their critique focused on the central committee's ability to limit direct action and local autonomy. The central committee could demand that any members justify their actions, and all locals had to have their propaganda (stickers, banners, and so on) approved by it. This was a big step for an organization based on street activism, in which each member carried a high degree of self-responsibility. For some members, a central committee contradicted these principles.

The introduction of a central committee reflected the changes and the generational shift occurring in RF. The arguments for the central committee were that it would make work within the organization more efficient, that it would make the organization appear more coherent to the public, that the activities of the locals would be more in tune with one another, and that the collective identity of RF would be strengthened, since quite a few members felt that this identity had been weakened in recent years.

It might be that the central committee suited the interests of a big, well-functioning local like the one in Gothenburg better than a local such as the one in Stockholm. In any case, former RF members recall the effects of the central committee on the organization differently: Some say that it hardly made a difference, others think that it was positive, and others believe it led to the organization's downfall.

MEMORY "WE TAUNTED THE NAZIS, AS THEY LAY ON THE PAVEMENT GETTING KICKED."

"The National Democrats held an election campaign rally in a suburb of Gothenburg. In left-wing circles, people spoke of the "first official Nazi event in Gothenburg in years." The antifascist movement had won many victories, and we, RF Gothenburg, felt strong. But we also saw rising repression across the country. We knew that there'd be plenty of cops at the event, and we prepared ourselves by strategically hiding projectiles—glass bottles, firecrackers, flares, things the police would take as soon as they searched us—near the square where the rally was held. But when we checked the hiding places on the day of the rally, they were empty. There was nothing for us to do but join the ranks of the protesters empty-handed. This was a clear failure. The only militant antifascist mini-happening that day was the attempt to pull a disoriented Nazi over the police barricades to our side, but he was saved by the cops, who pointed their guns at us.

A comrade and I were just about to head home and contemplate whether there was still anything useful to do that day when a former militant antifa told us to check on two fellows who were sneaking around our rally. The two were members of the National Youth Association,[12] a short-lived group close to ND. It seemed that they quickly noticed our—extremely discreet!—scouts, as they soon headed back to their car. Why they didn't go to the police asking for protection, rather than heading down a long, deserted street, we'll never know. We followed them, again very discreetly: in pairs, one after the other, in a long row. The Nazis met their fate in the parking lot. We took the hats of their organization as souvenirs. In the meantime, the cops were facing chants at the rally! We taunted the Nazis, as they lay on the pavement getting kicked, because of their martial arts training—it hadn't helped much.

—Written by a former RF Gothenburg member

MEMORY "WE LEFT A TRAIL OF UNCONSCIOUS NAZIS IN THE TUNNEL."

There's a party for the autonomous left at Stockholm University. This is a time when drum 'n' bass parties are the backbone of fundraising within the autonomous left. In another part of town, in Årsta, the Nazis are having their own party.

We are a small group of comrades who are pissed off that almost all of the lefties prefer to dance and have a good time rather than come with us to bash up Nazis. When we arrive in Årsta, we are able to motivate a group of kickers to join us. Now we're at least a dozen people. We move toward the Gullmarsplan subway station. On the way, we pass an old cemetery with a park. Underneath the park is a mass grave, which many don't know. There's a tunnel underneath the subway tracks, and on the other side there's a forested area. In order to get to the Nazis' party, we have to go through the tunnel. A significant part of it is sealed off due to construction work. For a distance of almost a hundred yards, we have to move in single file between temporary board fences.

We see three Nazis on the other side of the tunnel, but they don't see us. Some trees have just been trimmed in the cemetery, so we grab a bunch of branches. Our plan is clear: We beat up the three Nazis, let them run back to the party crying and cause panic there, since RF is near. Voilà, the Nazis' evening is ruined!

We move as inconspicuously through the tunnel as possible and put on our masks. We see that the three Nazis are joined by two more, but we don't care. Two more Nazis arrive, and we still don't care. And then another thirty arrive! It's the entire SMR gang on their way home.[13] They see us right away.

We are caught in the tunnel between the boards, as the Nazis run toward us. The one who reaches us first is high as a kite; his eyes look cartoonish. He holds a screwdriver in his hand, but we flatten him fast with the help of our branches. Then the next wave comes. The way through the tunnel is so narrow that we manage to keep the Nazis at bay with our improvised clubs. But since they all carry knives, we have to move backward. Reaching the exit of the tunnel takes two to three minutes, during which we do nothing but wildly swing those damn branches. When we're finally out of the tunnel, we have flattened so many of them that none of the others dare to follow us. So we walk back to the cemetery.

It wasn't a clear-cut victory, since we had to retreat. But the Nazis didn't dare leave the tunnel, none of us had to go to the hospital, and none of us got arrested—which wasn't the case with regard to the Nazis! Plus, we left a trail of unconscious Nazis in the tunnel. (It should be noted that they were grown men and we a bunch of seventeen-year-olds.)

—Told by a former RF Stockholm member

MEMORY "TIMES HAD CHANGED, AND ANTIFASCIST ACTIVISM ON THE STREETS HAD BROUGHT RESULTS: THE FASCISTS HARDLY DARED LEAVE THEIR HOLES."

"I think it was my first action in Stockholm. We had received information that the Nordic Youth had planned a flash mob somewhere in town. I was seventeen years old and had maybe attended one RF lecture, but I came from a self-organized antifa youth group in the Mälaren Valley and grew up in a small town with many Nazis, so I had plenty of experience with violence.

I had first got in touch with RF when an older comrade and I ran into two or three comrades from RF Gothenburg. RF Gothenburg had the reputation of being particularly well organized and particularly reckless. The myth surrounding RF relied heavily on half-fabricated stories that were retold over and over again: comrades who flattened in (more or less) spectacular fashion hordes of Nazis (with the comrades, of course, always being outnumbered); Nazis who were lured into traps by fake recruits; fascists who used their girlfriends as living shields and who saved their own skin by leaving their pals crying in the hands of antifascists. As a teenager, I could not get enough of these stories. Where I grew up, the 1990s lasted much longer than anywhere else. As a lefty punk, I was a constant target, and the RF Gothenburg folks were my heroes.

We were about fifteen people in Stockholm that day. The Nordic Youth were a bunch of fools. Boys with Burberry horse jackets who danced to hard bass and handed out calling cards. But they were a growing force within the White Power scene, a forerunner of what would later be known as the "alt-right." They talked about culture wars and adopted artistic expressions such as graffiti and hip-hop. They claimed to be anticapitalist and had, very clumsily, reached out to the autonomous left a few years before with the intention to form a cross-ideological alliance against capital. No one saw them as a threat on the streets.

We split into two groups, moving on opposite sides of the road. We walked as casually as possible and never lost sight of each other. I remember that my feet got wet. It was a warm winter day and very slushy. Our mood changed constantly, depending on the latest news from the scouts. Anxious one minute, on standby the next. A comrade said that we shouldn't expect too much. "These days, there's one brawl for twenty attempts." Times had changed, and antifascist activism on the streets had brought results: The fascists hardly dared leave their holes.

We hear that the scouts have spotted the Nordic Youth in the posh Östermalm neighborhood. About twenty-five of them are moving toward the Royal Gardens. There are eight of us in my group, and we are very close. The scouts are right behind the Nazis, who are moving toward us. Now there is plenty of anxiety. We are like a pack of hungry wolves and make a fast decision: We won't wait for the others, we will attack at the first best opportunity.

We are waiting behind a corner. Some of us put on masks. A well-trained comrade from Gothenburg wears a camouflage one. A comrade from Stockholm picks up a big pane of glass leaning against a garbage bin. My adrenaline goes nuts. An older comrade squeezes my shoulder and shakes me. His hand is all cramped because of the adrenaline. He grins and whispers, "Now it's on, goddamn it!" He probably remembers his first time.

We hear them come closer. I almost explode because of the adrenaline. A few seconds later, we can see them. When they're about a yard away, we jump around the corner and block their way. One of us grabs a Nazi by the collar; another punches him right away. The comrade from Stockholm with the glass pane raises it above his head and throws it at the Nazis, who are now full of fear. The pane shatters and there's broken glass everywhere. There isn't much space between the houses on one side of the pavement and the parked cars on the other. The comrade from Gothenburg with the camo mask is right at the front. I see only one Nazi who resists. He is frail and has the face of a child. The comrade from Gothenburg picks him up and throws him over his head back to us. Then our man from Gothenburg suddenly has the Nazis' boom box in his hand (they had probably brought it for the flash mob) and hits the Nazis with it. He looks like a caveman who has replaced a wooden club with a boom box. An older comrade from Stockholm sizes up a Nazi and says, "Shall *I* be fighting *you*?"

Taunting our opponents was as much a part of the RF myth as shrugging your shoulders in the face of danger. We spent a lot of time thinking about good one-liners during confrontations with Nazis. It was a part of dehumanizing them, which was necessary for what we did. Sometimes Nazis cried and begged for their lives. But antifascist violence was a kind of sport to us, a game, and trivializing it was part of that. We wanted to appear stone cold. As "psychopaths," which was always considered a compliment in RF circles.

The suffering of the Nordic Youth comes to an end when we hear the sirens of police cars. Their group is now significantly smaller—about half of them bailed at first contact. The

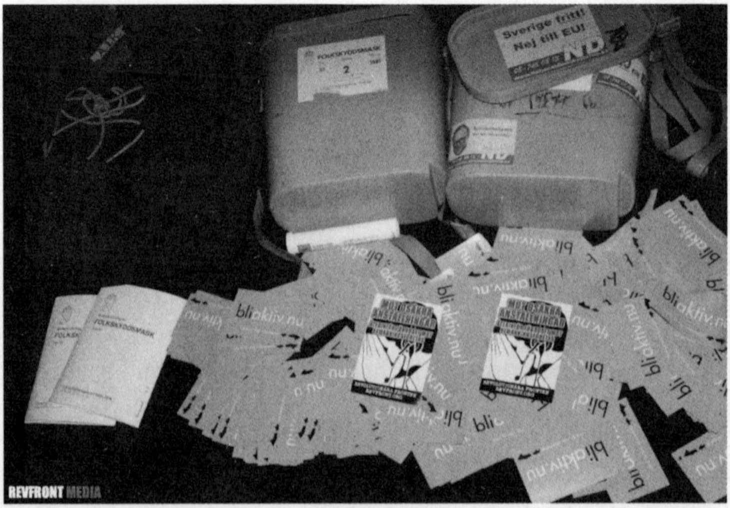

Contents of the seized Nordic Youth backpack.

other half isn't in good shape. Their clothes are torn and their noses bloody. One of them threw his backpack at us in panic. I take it with me. I run around two corners together with an older comrade, and then we slowly walk into a shopping mall, checking out clothes. I don't remember for how long. I was floating a few inches above the ground because of all the endorphins. I could hardly believe what had happened. My first fight with the Nordic Youth! Many would follow, until they disappeared from Stockholm—thanks to us.

Eventually, we all reunite. The group who missed the fight is disappointed. Our group is ecstatic, because it was a complete triumph. I am asked to carry the backpack home with me and make a photo of the contents together with an RF sticker against a neutral background. We want to prove that the contents are in our possession. The backpack contained the following: two big plastic containers, one hundred calling cards of the website bliaktiv.nu (Get Active, Now!), and medication for stomach acid. The last became a source of much scorn and ridicule. I found it very satisfying on a personal level to get ahold of the Nazi's valued property.

I remember many details of that day very clearly, although almost fifteen years have passed. Of course, my recollection is only a fraction of everything that happened. And how I remember things might have changed over the years. But I have stored the day as a great victory in my street-fighting memory—as one of the days we ought to remind ourselves of over and over again.

—*Written by a former RF Örebro member*

MEMORY "IT'S LIKE SOMEONE IS PULLING A SWITCH AND YOUR ENTIRE BODY IS FILLED WITH ADRENALINE; YOU FEEL TOGETHERNESS AND THAT YOU AND YOUR CREW ARE THE BEST, IMMORTAL."

"In the early 2010s, aging football hooligans in England founded an anti-Muslim movement, the English Defence League (EDL). The movement spread to various European countries, but none of those branches reached the numbers and the violent potential of the English original. The EDL claimed to be antiracist. They showed the Star of David at rallies and had a few nonwhite fellows marching along. All just for show. Their leader, Tommy Robinson, was a kind of right-wing influencer, but he was so uncouth that he could only mobilize a motley crew of drunks, losers, and idiots. The hopes of the EDL to build a strong, global hooligan movement died within a year.

The Swedish branch, the Swedish Defence League (SDL), was led by a man from Katrineholm who was easy to recognize because of his paper-thin build. He wore suits and hats that were at least three sizes too big. It is still incomprehensible to me how this fellow came to be the leader of a network of racist football hooligans.

The few rallies that the SDL had organized up to that point had been pitiful events with old hicks in wheelchairs, perhaps accompanied by a handful of wannabe hooligans in

Harrington jackets. But now they had mobilized for a big rally in Stockholm with visitors from various European branches, including the English original.

An AFA comrade had been in touch with the SDL leader for some time. He pretended to be a possible recruit, interested but shy. Before the rally in Stockholm, the SDL was careful with sharing information, but the night before, the AFA comrade got an invitation to a meeting of the organizing group, at 8 a.m. behind the Culture House in the center of Stockholm. There, the Swedes were supposed to meet the delegation from England. We quickly put together a group of ten reliable comrades. What follows is the story of that day.

We meet shortly before 7 a.m. on Sergels Torg, the square next to the Culture House. Sleepily, we stand in a half circle underneath the roof that covers a part of the square. We plan our attack and decide on a meeting point thereafter. Suddenly, we all simultaneously notice a tall man in our midst whom none of us knows. He doesn't say anything as we all stare at him quietly. Then he apologizes, shows us a plastic bag with perfume and lotion, and asks politely if we want to buy any of it. It's a special moment to see a junkie offer perfume he has probably stolen from one of the department stores nearby to a group of lads hanging out chatting, even being polite enough not to interrupt. We kindly refuse the offer, and he thanks us and walks away.

We divide into pairs and go to the Nazis' meeting place. Most of the actions we did in Stockholm at the time, we did with AFA. We knew each other well, everyone was reliable, and we were always hungry.

A comrade and I are in the lead; the next pair follows twenty yards behind us. We know that SDL consists of clowns, but we are not sure about the Englishmen. If they have experienced hooligans among them, we must be on our toes, especially if they are many.

We see a group of men standing on a patch of grass, about fifteen to twenty of them. We are across the street. The comrade I'm with has plenty of experience and is infamous among the Nazis. I have great trust in him. Instead of waiting for the rest of the group, he puts on his gloves and crosses the street. I follow. Some Nazis check us out. I'm under the impression that the rest of us are still far away, which concerns me a little, but suddenly they are right by our side.

When we reach the Nazis, my friend asks in a voice reminiscent of Ronny and Ragge, "Hi, guuuys, are you here to deeemonstrate?"[14] One of the Nazis seems to understand what's coming. He is shaking his head and takes a couple of steps back. The Nazi my friend directed the question to proves to be one of the Englishmen. He manages to say, "Sorry?" right before he is hit in the face. I grab another Nazi by the collar while the rest of them run. The Nazi I'm holding is trying to get away too, which means that his T-shirt is soon shredded. We only get a few punches in before all of the Nazis are gone. They leave a paper bag with propaganda, which unfortunately we can't carry with us. We leave without a scratch. "That was easy."

We have planned actions with more comrades later in the day. We are about sixty people, which is a lot for the time, certainly more than average. I don't recall the numbers from the Nazis' rally, but it must have been fifty to a hundred, including drunks and pensioners.

We spend the day in the Liljeholmen neighborhood. We have a few scouts roaming the city. Every now and again we receive information, but nothing substantial. The day is reaching its end, and some of us are already on the way home. The AFA comrade whom the SDL leader invited to the morning meeting tries to reach him one more time. More as a joke, since it must be obvious to SDL now that he is not the potential recruit he claims to be.

Officially, actions are over for the day, but since many of the out-of-towners, especially from Gothenburg, stay overnight, there are still twenty to twenty-five of us. We hear the SDL leader's phone ring and make silly jokes, like a group of kids doing prank calls (which we are, in a way). To our great surprise, the SDL leader answers. The AFA comrade quickly retreats to a corner and talks to him. We are laughing silently, mouths wide open but not making a sound.

A minute later, the AFA comrade puts down the phone and comes over. He has told the SDL leader that he slept in, missed the morning meeting, and then couldn't get past the protesters in order to attend the rally. The SDL leader said that our comrade got lucky, because the morning meeting got attacked; somehow, he explained, the antifascists must have got word of the meeting. Our comrade expressed relief that he wasn't there. Then our Trojan horse was invited to the Broder Tuck pub in the Södermalm neighborhood, where the SDL leader was apparently having a few beers with his lieutenant and the leader of the Polish Defence League. Our AFA comrade promised to be there in half an hour.

A familiar feeling spread among us like wildfire. Even years later, I still feel it when I recall moments like this. It is difficult to describe, but everyone who has ever been in a similar situation knows it: wound-up, manic, nervous, euphoric, all at once. It's like someone is pulling a switch and your entire body is filled with adrenaline; you feel togetherness and that you and your crew are the best, immortal. When I think about my time in RF, I still feel that way. And so I did that day in 2013.

We send scouts to the pub. They see patrol cars in the vicinity. Nothing odd about that, it is a Saturday afternoon. We decide not to attack inside the pub but at the first best opportunity outside. We will simply follow them.

We enter the pub, try to avoid any attention, and spread out. At least the staff must have found it odd that there were suddenly twenty kids occupying ten tables and ordering five soft drinks. The Nazis sit at a private table in a corner, just four or five of them. All losers. After about ten minutes, they go outside to smoke. As if on cue, we all rise and follow.

Outside, we form a circle around them. They quickly notice that something is not right. The bouncer approaches us but gets a feisty response from a young Stockholm comrade who has not made a particular impression until now: "Fuck off, or you'll be next!" The bouncer goes back into the pub and locks the door.

The SDL leader tries to smoke a cigarette. His hands are trembling. Some of us have gathered around just him. One of us smacks the cigarette out of his mouth. He tries to ignore that and gets another cigarette from his pack. A comrade is taking the pack. The Nazi trembles more and more; there doesn't seem to be any strength in his frail body. I take his hat and put it on. He stares into nothingness. Maybe he is fearing for his life. Comrades now empty his pockets, take his phone, taunt him. He cries for help, but his voice is so weak that no one hears him. We laugh. He is such a pitiful fellow that he is hardly worth a beating—a freak who gets to experience for the first time how we treat Nazis. Finally, one of his pals gets involved and is trying to pull him out of our circle. Not a good idea. He probably gets the hardest slap in the face he ever got. Bleeding from the nose, he yells, "Police, help, help!"

We leave it there and take off in different directions. I am with two other comrades and am still wearing the SDL leader's silly hat. One of my comrades puts his sunglasses on upside down and wears his baseball cap crooked. He intends to appear like a drunk or a disabled person—someone who could not possibly have been involved in a street fight.

During the following days, the SDL leader gets a lot of criticism from Nazis on Facebook because he has allowed "communist wankers" to humiliate him. His excuses are hilarious. He claims that he wore a suit that was too tight (his suits were always way too big) and that he didn't feel "the adrenaline flow." He was unable to keep his position in the SDL. Soon thereafter, the group was gone.

—Written by a former RF Örebro member

MALMÖ AND MORE ABOUT THE MACHO CRITIQUE

"

I liked "No class, only style." And I liked that they spoke about your mother when they spoke about women's liberation. They had a different way to say things. It wasn't like in the leftist swamp, where everyone just throws opinions at you. "You men, you!" I liked the way that RF did it, but I wasn't very well read either.

"We Were Too Macho, We Were Too This or That, We Were Wearing the Wrong Clothes"

RF had plans to found a group in Skåne, but it never really got off the ground before RF dissolved in 2015. The biggest fascist threat in Malmö, Skåne's capital, was the now defunct Party of the Swedes.

The people who wanted to found an RF local in Malmö had been active in leftist groups for a few years but never felt really comfortable there. When they were very young, they wanted to join AFA because they had fought Nazis together with AFA members. They were refused membership, apparently because they were too young. But years later, after RF's dissolution, they were told that this hadn't been the real reason; the real reason, the AFA folks now said, was that they were too unschooled politically and not "politically correct." In the following interview, two of them share their perspective:

Tell us about joining RF!

1: I was already active, but not organized. I was all over the place.

2: Yes, we popped up here and there.

1: That's how we got to know each other, although we went to the same school. We started to have more contact after meeting at a Kristallnacht memorial event.

2: But we weren't in any groups, we were independent.

1: Later, we founded a group called the "Revolutionary Youth." That must have been in 2010 or 2011.

2: We already knew about RF back then.

1: We had seen all the videos!

2: We just thought, "This is the shit!" But we weren't organized yet.

1: Even though I grew up with politics. I started to go to demonstrations at the age of fifteen. Together with two friends, I wanted to join AFA, but they said we were too young.

2: It wasn't easy here.

1: We *were* too young. But later, they talked to me again, after many years. And they kind of apologized, saying that they hadn't been honest with us. They could have said, "Look, the way you're acting now, you can't join us, but if you go through some political schooling, it might be possible." You know?

2: Yes, but there you see the difference between RF and AFA. AFA can't take care of the youth. We were like kickers. At least I was, I had no education. I mean, they did invite us to meetings, with Mangla for example.[1]

1: But that wasn't much fun.

2: I understand that AFA saw us as kids. We really weren't very old.

1: In any case, in 2011 we got in touch with RF through the Revolutionary Youth. We invited them to give lectures and such.

2: Yes, and I think that same year we applied for membership in RF Gothenburg.

Did you try to join another AFA group?

1: They were weird. Lots of discussions. They didn't like us.

2: No, they really didn't. At least that's how it felt.

1: They outed us on Facebook. "Shit, now RF is in town!" Stuff like that.

2: They didn't like our attitude. I'm sure we were macho, but they also felt challenged because we were independent. AFA had controlled the antifascist scene in Skåne for many years. There weren't any other antifa groups, and I'm sure that AFA didn't want to have any others around either. I like the AFA folks in Skåne, but I only came to appreciate them later, when I understood the circumstances better.

1: Sure. I think we could have collaborated more with them. But they didn't make it easy for us.

2: They would probably say the same about us. But you find these problems everywhere. And the situation in Lund is different, although it is very close to Malmö.

1: In Lund, there were also people who wanted to join RF.

What were the reasons that made you apply for membership in RF?

2: There was no other way for us to be organized. We were not welcome in any other group.

1: Correct. And we didn't want to be part of the leftist swamp where everyone always just complained about us.

2: Indeed.

1: We were too macho, we were too this or that, we were wearing the wrong clothes. They didn't like anything about us.

2: In Malmö, we were rejected. AFA was different from RF, they presented themselves very differently. Think of the RF videos, for example. RF was about being tough. So why did we want to join RF? There weren't many alternatives. And we thought they were more badass than any of the others—or at least I did.

1: There was a romanticization of violence.

2: Yes, there was, let's be honest. "The harder, the better."

"It is about . . . your mother." Gothenburg, March 8, 2010.

1: I liked "No class, only style." And I liked that they spoke about your mother when they spoke about women's liberation. They had a different way to say things. It wasn't like in the leftist swamp, where everyone just throws opinions at you. "You men, you!" I liked the way that RF did it, but I wasn't very well read either.

2: In my opinion, the movement in Malmö is quite different from that in Stockholm, Gothenburg, or even Halmstad.[2] In Malmö, there are high expectations when it comes to education. You have to have attended university. In the beginning, we didn't understand that, because we don't come from that milieu and we were very young.

1: That's right.

2: At the same time, none of the groups in Malmö offered any education for their members. You were expected to already know everything when you joined them and to simply swallow all the opinions you were fed. But you don't have to agree on everything just because you share similar values. There should be possibilities to get educated! Kudos to RF Gothenburg, they took the time to help us educate ourselves. It couldn't have been easy! But they really tried to create a space for working-class people, including those who didn't fit anywhere else. By the way, that's crazy that AFA later apologized to you!

1: Isn't it?

Do you think that the macho critique of RF was justified?

1: Well …

2: What shall I say? In some sense maybe. There's a special vibe when guys with a certain attitude get together. It can get macho.

1: It can get to be too much.

2: Even I thought that it was a bit too much sometimes. We could have been more chill. At the same time, I found the critique exaggerated. It seemed that they always wanted to find something about us that was wrong, and the macho thing was easy to call out. That's why they always came back to it, even though we did plenty of good work.

1: True. The critique focused on antifascism. But we did a housing campaign in Gothenburg, and in Malmö we targeted the employment office. There was plenty of other stuff we did, but they focused on the macho bits, and perhaps on what they perceived as self-righteousness on our part. There was some truth to that, but it was also a feature that attracted many to RF. And the macho thing might have been necessary. Without the hard rhetoric, we might have been less successful.

2: That's true, that's a central question.

1: Later, in Malmö, we were called macho just because we pumped iron and did martial arts. But nowadays, many do that![3] So was the macho critique justified? Yes and no. Were we self-righteous? Yes, sometimes, at least I was.

2: But there was a lot of exaggeration. From both sides.

1: Once, I was asked to leave a party because I was macho. I mean, at that point you exclude people just because they are different. I hadn't done anything.

When you became RF members, did the reality of the organization fit the image you had?

2: The image we had came from the propaganda. But, yes, I think it was what I had expected.

1: Me too. RF members were always ready, never pulled back, they were very experienced, and they gave us a great education.

2: There was a clear structure and you could get educated.

Can you say something about RF Halmstad? Was it an official local?

2: Yes, but at the very end of RF. I was no longer particularly active then.

1: I was part of that local!

2: All the members from Skåne were supposed to join, but I was living in Gothenburg at the time.

How many members were there in Skåne?

2: In the beginning, we were three, then four, then five. And there were those—what were they called?

1: Hangarounds.

2: Yes, hangarounds. With them, we were maybe ten.

1: Max. Not many in any case, and some only stayed briefly.

2: Full members, we were only a handful.

The AFA groups in Skåne weren't very happy that there were RF members in the region. While the left in other regions of Sweden had grudgingly come to accept RF, in Skåne they were still rejected. The high level of education that was expected from left-wing activists might have been one reason, but the RF members from Skåne interviewed for this book were disappointed that so little attention was paid to RF's political work. To many, the rejection of RF seemed to be a matter of principle. This wasn't entirely unknown in other regions, though. As the interviews conducted for this book confirm, RF members didn't feel fully accepted by the left anywhere, which added to the pride they felt about their own organization. Another former member from Skåne speaks about his experiences in the following interview:

I was probably one of the few RF members who had already been active in autonomous leftist groups before I joined RF. In my hometown, four or five of us formed an SUF chapter, and when I moved to Malmö, I was active in migrant justice projects and a member of No One Is Illegal and Action Against Deportation.

In 2012, one of my old friends became a member of RF Örebro. I visited the RF comrades there over a weekend and got a very good impression. I still remember that weekend fondly. We looked at online videos of Nazis getting beaten up in London. The RF Örebro folks were obsessed with antifascism.

That same year, I went to a demonstration in Eskilstuna. The Party of the Swedes and their youth organization wanted to celebrate May 1 there. We were twenty black bloc kids, and we managed to get through the police barriers and attack the Nazis. But since hardly anyone else came along, we were pushed back. I had to go to the hospital because I got a bottle to my head. After that experience, I made the conclusion that I either couldn't do that kind of stuff or that I had to do it with people who knew what they were doing. In Eskilstuna, the Nazis had been better prepared for a physical confrontation than us. They had batons and masks. We were only kids disliking Nazis. After some consideration, I told my friend in Örebro that I also wanted to join. This was right around the time when Kärrtorp and March 8 in Malmö happened.[4] In Skåne, the Party of the Swedes was a real threat.

Why didn't you join AFA? How did it compare to your image of RF?

My image of RF was formed during the time I considered getting organized. AFA was never an option. I felt closer to RF because my friend was there. There was also this story about two young antifas who had been rejected by AFA. They were told that they were too young, but they suspected that their rejection had to do with social and cultural reasons.

What was your image of RF like?
It seemed that they were taking activism more seriously than others. It seemed like a natural step for me to join them after years in other groups. I had turned twenty at the time and was too old for the various youth associations. Quite a lot of people stopped doing politics at that age, or they joined the Left Party. But some wanted to continue doing antifa work, and I was one of them.

In 2010, we went to Stockholm because of the Salem March, and in the inner city there was a bit of a scuffle between SUF and the cops. My very first impression of RF probably comes from that day. While SUF and the cops were having a bit of a back-and-forth, a bigger group of folks watched nearby from a stairway. Rumors spread that Nazis were observing the demonstration. But it turned out that they were from RF. That stuck with me. And then there was the way that SUF talked about RF: RF members looked like Nazis, they talked like Nazis, they despised the left, and they loved violence. In short, they were pretty much Nazis themselves. That framed my image of RF in the beginning, but when I actually met RF members, that image changed completely. Yes, there was a romanticization of violence, but at the core of RF was class politics. RF had a kind of class consciousness I have never encountered in the left otherwise. RF was a class organization—and they beat up Nazis.

Was it mostly about class consciousness, or was there concrete political work attached to it?
Class consciousness was central, but there was concrete action. To begin with, in RF, class consciousness was tied to antifascism, because Nazis were seen as class traitors. It was this hatred that drove RF. We didn't care so much about what

the Nazis thought, which opinions they held, it was more of an "us against them" mentality. We represented the class, they represented something else. We despised the Nazis for betraying the class.

Was that class consciousness particularly tangible within the organization?
Maybe. There are RF articles that explain how capitalism divides the working class and leads some workers to turn against their own. But you probably needed to be a member to understand how class identity determined everything in RF. It also meant that RF talked about fascism in a way that no other group did. The classical understanding of fascism, also within the left, was that Nazis were evil people with evil ideas. But for RF, all that mattered were class relationships. Did fascists act as strikebreakers? Did capitalists hire fascists to turn against protesters? It was a widespread view within RF that Nazis fought the left in the interests of the powerful, and that they were lackeys of the ruling class.

Do you think RF was misunderstood by the left?
I'm not sure if I would put it that way. RF didn't make much of an effort to be understood. RF didn't care much about the left. It took a lot of time and energy to make yourself understood to everyone, and that was not a priority for RF. We instead dedicated our time and energy to other things.

Can you say a bit more about the fascist scene in Malmö?
When I became an RF member, there was, first and foremost, the Party of the Swedes and its unofficial youth organization, the National Youth Association. NMR had no activists in Malmö, only in the countryside.[5] The main threat came from the Party of the Swedes and the circles around Andreas Carlsson, who had attended weapons training with nationalist groups in Ukraine before severely injuring comrades on March 8, 2014.[6] Then there was the security deputy of the

Party of the Swedes, who lived in Limhamn, and some kids who hung out with the fascists among Malmö FF supporters.

Was the Party of the Swedes active on the streets?
Not officially. But one reason for its demise was internal conflicts. Many of their members had come from NSF. They were street activists, and they wanted to continue to be, but the party leadership pursued a different image now, focusing on leafleting and running in elections. This tension could not be overcome. The party leadership even glossed over the home visits that party members got, which also meant that they didn't get any support from the party. Therefore, most of them stopped being active, or they went to NMR.

It seems like you were well informed about the inner workings of the party.
Yes, I think we had a pretty good understanding. In general, AFA did better research than us, but we had some good people too.

Did you not receive information from AFA?
There was exchange, but it was more based on personal relationships, not so much on any official collaboration. I think that AFA Malmö approached us with sympathetic caution. I know that some comrades have a very negative image of AFA, but I had friends in AFA and believe that they kept a distance from RF mainly for security reasons. They saw us as crazy kids who would end up in prison. Well, they weren't wrong, were they?

THE REPRESSION IS TAKING A TOLL

"

In the beginning, the cops didn't care about us, and not about the Nazis either. They liked neither us nor them—even though there were cops who were Nazis too. But by and large, we could do what we wanted. The cops didn't care when we got a hiding, and they didn't care when the Nazis got one. You had to be really stupid or really unlucky to get arrested. That changed, drastically, under the Reinfeldt government.

Kärrtorp, Operation Eskil, and Repression

In December 2013, an antifascist manifestation was held in Kärrtorp, a suburb of Stockholm. The reason was that the suburb had seen a drastic increase in Nazi graffiti over several weeks. Thirty minutes into the manifestation, it was attacked by thirty SMR members.[1] Antifa activists who were present managed to protect the crowd and chase the Nazis into the forest.

Four antifascists were put on trial. Even though none of them was a current RF member, RF received a lot of media attention, as two of them had been in RF before. Both had left the organization in 2009, during the generational shift. One of them was the anarchist Dennis Thelning, a member of the Little League. Dennis was charged with attempted murder and went underground. He was later arrested and acquitted after his charges had been dropped to aggravated assault. The court classified his actions as self-defense. This was not the case with

Dennis Thelning in hiding, 2014. "The truth will prevail." An inside message to a Nazi who was hiding at the same time.

the other former RF member, who was accused of attempted murder. He was sentenced to six and a half years in prison. The other two antifas were, like Dennis, acquitted. Dennis died a year after the trial, twenty-six years old.

The events of Kärrtorp received a lot of attention in Swedish media. Within the autonomous left—and beyond—the slogan "Antifascism Is Self-Defense" became highly popular. The media mainly reported about "two extremist groups clashing," which is a gross simplification of what happened. Eyewitnesses as well as video recordings prove that the Nazi attack that day went beyond the norm. Nobody who has properly studied the chain of events can deny that it was only because of the antifascists who were on site that no participants of the manifestation were seriously hurt. Among them were elderly people and toddlers. The police had no control over the situation. It was the antifascists who drove away the Nazis.

In the early morning hours of November 19, 2013, police conducted several raids in Swedish towns under the name "Operation Eskil." The target were alleged RF members. The police broke into apartments, ransacked them, and arrested eight people. Some of these people later received prison sentences. SÄPO agents assisted the prosecution and claimed that they had evidence for the RF membership of the accused, which is why the prosecution demanded particularly harsh sentences. SÄPO's alleged evidence was never presented in court.

Before Operation Eskil, there had been a change in Swedish law. Prisoners who were sentenced for political actions were put in the same category as gang members. But while members of the same gang were usually housed in the same unit, the antifascists were all separated.

Various media outlets followed Operation Eskil from the arrests to the prison sentences. *Aftonbladet* was present during the raids.[2] The paper published photographs of people being led to police cars in handcuffs. It is unlikely these photos could have been taken had the paper not been tipped off by police.

The media and the police seemed to agree that the events of Kärrtorp and Operation Eskil led to the dissolution of RF in the fall of 2015. There might be some truth to that, but it's not the whole truth.

RF Faces a Junction

With the generational shift in RF, discussions about the future of the organization started. Many members thought that it wasn't sustainable to pursue two different paths at once: class politics on the one hand, with delegates attending meetings of leftist networks, and militant antifascism, in clandestine groups, on the other. Not least due to the growing repression, it became increasingly difficult to hold both wings together. Some members also felt that a long-term strategy was lacking. They felt that RF had methods but no common strategy to reach the goal of a classless society.

One solution that was discussed was to strictly separate both wings in practical terms but to keep a common administrative structure. A relevant motion was filed at a nationwide meeting, with the proponents citing examples such as the Black Panthers, the Irish liberation movement, and the animal rights movement. The motion did not pass.

The problem of negotiating two main tendencies within the organization was not new. Minutes from a nationwide meeting in 2006 summarize how the organization approached the issue at the time:

> With regard to how to present the organization in public: Some members think that we should not address certain questions under the name RF at all. But the majority thinks that it is not a problem for RF to address most issues. We can do militant actions in the name of RF and distribute leaflets and have open assemblies at the same time. The only relevant question is what's best for the organization. Many members say that they enjoy distributing leaflets. RF is a broad organization. There is room for members to get involved in things other than militant antifascism. If members want to avoid being branded as a militant RF member in public, they can articulate themselves accordingly. Again, the only relevant question is what's best for the organization; that must always determine the actions of all RF members. What others think is of no interest.

This was an accepted view during the entire lifetime of RF. But as we have seen in the interviews conducted for this book, the growing repression made it increasingly difficult to keep a healthy balance between militancy and other work. Many members thought that the balancing act was starting to take a toll, which in turn led to tensions within the organization.

2014–2015

THE END

RF Dissolves

In Gothenburg, where RF had been founded, discussions about a possible dissolution of RF were the most frequent. The reasons were the increasing difficulties in keeping both wings of the organization together, the growing repression, and the fact that several members were now serving prison sentences.

RF Gothenburg was still the biggest local, where the separation between the militant and the political wing was most tangible. Some members grew increasingly frustrated because actions they wanted to do were questioned due to security reasons. They decided to either leave the organization or propose its dissolution. They chose the latter. As they explained in interviews for this book, this had a lot to do with pride and the RF spirit. They did not want to leave the organization in the hands of new members who, from their perspective, didn't share it. Furthermore, they deemed it better to actively and officially dissolve the organization rather than let it fizzle out. This, they reckoned, was happening with AFA. In the motion proposing the dissolution, they formulated this as follows:

> We never wanted to be part of the left, but we made many compromises. Eventually, this led to an identity crisis, a catch-22 moment: "Who are we?" Instead of seizing new terrain, we became yet another leftist group that spends most of its time in meetings and is little more than a

paper tiger. Today, we have members who may participate in three or four actions a year. Only recently, we would have laughed at such a lack of dedication. This is what we considered the rest of the left to be like, but not us! In our opinion, we must recognize that we have now become part of the left we used to hate. Therefore, our organization has lost its purpose.

An RF founding member recalls the nationwide meeting where the motion was passed:

> As far as I recall, a number of members were against it, particularly from Stockholm. But many were for it, and some abstained from voting. This was, of course, a tough decision for everyone. You don't do anything like that lightheartedly. Some changed their opinion during the meeting. Many of us had given much of our lives to RF, but I think most had gotten to a point where we felt we were no longer moving forward, so they thought it was better if people were free to turn to other things.

One of the members who was pushing for the dissolution recalls the time leading up to the meeting in the following interview:

> The initiative came from a few people in Hammarkullen. They were a little bitter and ... well, I think it was two things: first, the division between antifascism and the other political work; second, the division between Stockholm and, well, pretty much everyone else.
>
> A year earlier, a motion had been filed to create two parts of the organization. It wasn't very well written, but it focused on an obvious problem—namely, that it was no longer sustainable to be "half-open." On the one hand, we had delegates at network meetings with thirty participants from different leftist groups, and on the other hand, we uploaded videos in which people got their heads kicked in. At some

point, that was no longer feasible. What are you going to discuss at those network meetings? How are you going to collaborate with other groups?

When we proposed a two-tier organization, we didn't necessarily think that the political wing should turn down the rhetoric. We considered the RF rhetoric very important, because you didn't find that anywhere else in the left. We looked at what the Animal Rights Alliance was doing.[1] They had a wing doing outreach with much public support, but they also had a militant wing operating under the cover of darkness. They managed to unite both. We were inspired by that, but our motion was voted down. For Linköping and Örebro, a division made no sense, because the locals were too small. And Stockholm had a different view.

Okay. But why dissolve the organization rather than leave and found your own antifa group?

We gave ourselves some time after the motion proposing a division was rejected, but we grew ever more bitter, because we felt that an increasing number of members dedicated way too little time to RF. They were simply much less active than we were. Repression in Gothenburg was less heavy than in other places. Yes, I was arrested during the raids as well. They stormed my apartment with weapons drawn, and it does something to you, you become paranoid. The psychological consequences are greater than after being stabbed. But it hardly changed my political work. Others, however, got scared only hearing about the raids. For example, they wanted for us to no longer do home visits. There was increasing tension between the antifa group and the rest, and when that tension grew deeper, we pretty much started to do our own thing. In the end, we pretty much operated independently. We felt excluded, and many of us were probably burned out. Increasingly, dissolution seemed like the only sensible choice.

Then came the day when lectures for RF members had been organized in Gothenburg. Everyone came, including the members from Stockholm. But the night before, there was a big antifa action in Stockholm, in which people from other groups and independents participated. RF Stockholm had been invited, but they had declined, apparently because of security reasons. Some RF Gothenburg members joined nonetheless. It was a great action! Yet afterward, we were criticized for having taken part, also in Gothenburg. The Stockholm local probably felt that we had disrespected them, but we considered it ludicrous to travel to Gothenburg for lectures while missing a great antifa action at home. Neither side backed down, and the conflict escalated. My feeling was: "What do I do in an organization where I get criticized for joining a badass antifa action, which the others don't want to join because they would rather listen to bloody lectures? How can these people and I work in the same organization?" So now me and my closest comrades were totally convinced that we had to dissolve RF. Bringing together the militant and the political wings no longer seemed like an option. Eventually, the moment came when we said, "Okay, let's get this done."

Why did we not just leave? Pride. We talked about forming our own clandestine group. But pride got in the way. We had built RF. Should we now leave it to people who we thought sucked? In hindsight, I wouldn't say they all sucked, but at the time that was how I felt. At the time, I felt that we couldn't allow them to bury RF.

And then Gothenburg was for the dissolution and Stockholm against it?

Yes, you can put it that way. The motion came from Gothenburg, and so we had more time to discuss it. We thought it was important to dissolve the organization on our own terms, not least because of all the repression. AFA seemed to be just dying off. We thought a clear end was better, determined by ourselves. Restructuring the organization didn't seem to be an option. But I underestimated how big of a factor the burnout was.

> By the way, the first time we filed the motion to dissolve, it was rejected. That was in the spring of 2015. But we filed it again in the fall, and then it passed. The half year in between the two meetings was strange. For us, the dissolution was only a matter of time.

Here is another view on the dissolution:

> The repression was a big reason, we had cops on us all the time. If there were four of them at a protest earlier, there were now a hundred, plus plainclothes officers, plus helicopters. It had a big impact on us, especially the activism on the streets. The state did everything in its power to quell political violence, which meant that what we had built our reputation on was no longer doable. Or so went the argument of the proponents of dissolution. They said that RF was no longer able to play the same role as before, and that the old methods didn't make any sense if people got arrested all the time. We had long discussions about that. It was a big decision to dissolve, of course.
>
> ***But you voted for it?***
> Yes, I did, but I don't know if I would today. Today, I see both advantages and disadvantages with it. I'm not sure if it was the right thing to do. The stuff about repression, yes, that was correct, and I guess people assumed it wouldn't stop as long as certain individuals were associated with the organization. The police had learned a lot about RF. I think there was an understanding that it would be easier for these individuals to be active outside of RF, but after the dissolution most of them just disappeared. And with the organization, important resources disappeared. That could have been handled better.

Another member reflects on RF's methods and strategies, first pondering the question of whether there was a coherent understanding of them within the organization:

I would say there was, at least over a certain period. Toward the end, it might have only been so among the most active members. These members got increasingly frustrated, because they felt that the rest of the organization wasn't like them and how they had always wanted RF to be. That's why they had first pushed through the central committee: They thought everything would get better if they were just able to call the shots. But it never really worked that way, and so they pushed for the dissolution.

I would say that there had long been a healthy balance between a unified organization on the one hand and sufficient local autonomy on the other. I think the attempt to unify everything went against RF's internal culture. The biggest problem in my eyes was that the thing we were best at—militant antifascism on the streets—was no longer possible because of the repression. And in other things we simply weren't that good. That could have probably been changed, but it would have taken time.

In the beginning of RF, we had short-term goals: The Nazis had to be chased out of the streets. And we were very successful with that. But we weren't able to build a strong organization. I mean, not everything was bad. The campaign against jobbjakt.se was successful, we supported the garbage collector strike in Stockholm, we put class politics back on the agenda of the left. But there were lots of different opinions within the organization on how to go forward and improve the political work. RF was a blend of communists and anarchists. Early on, that didn't matter because street activism was the common denominator, but later it got more problematic.

Was it the activism on the streets that had held the organization together?

Yes, we did what needed to be done to get the Nazis off the streets. But then repression became too strong, and we should have eased off a little instead of publicly bragging

"Class against class."

about our actions. The media really exploited a particularly brutal video from the Mälaren Valley, which ended up as the centerpiece of the *Uppdrag Granskning* program.[2] Stuff like that was too provocative. I think we could have messed with the Nazis without advertising ourselves. But I was a strong opponent of the dissolution! RF should have continued. For all I cared, as a phantom! There were people who still wanted to do things. I mean, people spent years in prison and sacrificed their health for RF! The Nazis had great respect for the name. We could have made use of that. Sometimes it was enough to put a sticker on the apartment of a Nazi to make him leave the movement. You don't build a reputation like that overnight. I would have liked to see RF as a phantom. There were no good reasons for the dissolution.

What were the mistakes that RF made?
One mistake was to accept members only to grow. In the beginning, we had very strict criteria concerning membership, but then things got more lax. It also had to do with street fighting no longer being the only focus, so you no longer

> solely needed people fit for that purpose. But that change created tensions.
>
> Mistakes had already been made in the beginning, though. We should have made a bigger effort to bring women into the organization. The more time that passed, the more difficult it became to do something against the male dominance. I think that RF could have built its reputation even without grooming this super hard image. Speaking of macho culture. But we were all very young, hardly adults.

Below follows another perspective by a former member, this time again by a proponent of dissolution:

> For me, two things were crucial. The first one was a really unpleasant experience concerning repression. I will try to keep it short.
>
> NMR regularly distributed leaflets in Gothenburg. Those were "blitz actions," to avoid them being busted by antifas. But our research people were able to figure out a pattern, and they were pretty good at predicting when and where NMR would distribute their leaflets. And for messing with NMR, we could mobilize many experienced people.
>
> There was a day in 2014 when we expected them to go leafleting, and we gathered our crew. We shared all information personally, no phones. No one was allowed to bring phones to the action either. Only the prospects in Halmstad got an electronic message with information about the place and time for our prep meeting in the morning. That was it.
>
> At the morning meeting, we activated two brand-new telephones that we had just purchased. One went to the scouts, one stayed with the rest of us. The scouts went to where we expected NMR to show up. They sent a message after fifteen minutes: "They're in the parking lot unfolding their flags." We made our way there in small groups. It was a Saturday morning, the city was only just waking up. We saw no cops, everything was quiet. We had placed a bag

with masks and mouthguards at a strategic spot. One of the scouts was supposed to pick it up. But as he turned into the alley where the bag was placed, he heard a plainclothes cop speak into his phone: “Not yet! They have not picked up the masks yet.” Our comrade left the bag where it was and tried to call us—but our phone was dead! We were already near NMR and saw plainclothes cops everywhere. We had to call the action off.

As we were heading to our assembly point in small groups, we heard a helicopter, and suddenly there police vans everywhere. Me and the two comrades I was with sat down on a bench. Two women jogged past us. We said something like, “They didn’t look too bad.” Then they passed us again—and again! At that point, we thought, “This is nuts! We can no longer do this. No matter how hard we try, they are always a step ahead.”

So that was the first thing. The other was Operation Eskil. Of course that had an impact on me, it would be ridiculous to pretend that it didn’t. No one had expected the raids, at least not in the way they went down. They stormed into our apartments with weapons drawn! One comrade got arrested in a hut in the forest, where he was staying with some friends. The cops had run through the forest with their weapons. Many comrades were nervous and demoralized, and I felt that what we did no longer made any sense. The energy we needed for that kind of stuff was gone.

But it was mainly members from Gothenburg who voted for the dissolution, right? In Stockholm, people felt differently.

Yes, but we never understood why. The local in Stockholm wasn’t even that active. The way we saw it, the RF spirit was mainly alive in Gothenburg and Örebro. So why did Stockholm make a fuss? But maybe I underestimated how much RF meant even for them. For me, it meant a lot! I had no idea what I was supposed to do after RF. I joined when I was sixteen years old. I became an adult in RF. At certain times, my entire life consisted of RF, I had no social contacts outside of the organization. I met other members after work, we partied together, we beat up Nazis together. I still talk to former members about what went wrong. And when I think of all that, I do understand why some were against the dissolution. RF was a big part of our lives, and it defined our identity in a way you didn't find in other groups.

Are you now talking about the RF spirit?
Yes, it was fed to you. You carried it with you before you even joined the first action. Our form of activism demanded a lot from you as an individual, so the collective backing you up was essential. Herd instinct might have played into it, but a lot was about your personal self-esteem. When a new member had joined their first action, we drank and celebrated, they were embraced by everyone, the mood was festive, almost in a cheesy way, but it tied the organization together, and pretty much every single member became a great comrade. They are still socialists today, but hardly any of them is organized. I think the reason is that you don't find the same spirit anywhere else.

In the next interview, a member who was in RF for ten years shares their view of the dissolution and stresses the positive aspects of the organization:

It gave me a lot to put so much time and energy into politics. Politics still means a lot to me. I'm still a socialist, just like I was then. I am proud that we brought so many people to the organization who had always been told that they were fuckups. We did many positive things! I think most people who were involved in RF had the feeling that they grew personally.

So you think it's true what many say: RF brought people to political activism who might not have been active otherwise.

Yes, I think that's true. There is no comparable organization today. There is no organization that speaks to people in the same way, especially younger people. We had criteria for accepting new members, of course, but anyone was able to apply and come to our meetings. In that sense, there were no huge hurdles. It was the will that counted. Everything has advantages and disadvantages, but we had people come to us who had experienced plenty of violence in their lives and grown up under difficult circumstances. RF created a space where they felt accepted just the way they were, and where they could feel that they were making a positive contribution. I was never in any other organization, but I have enough insight into leftist groups to know that they are more elitist than what RF was. They exclude people. At times, someone would throw around big words even in RF, but in general RF was much closer to the life of ordinary people than what other leftist groups were.

How did you experience the dissolution?
Gothenburg was behind it. They filed the motion because they thought the organization was no longer serving any purpose and that it had turned into something it was never meant to be. That's how they explained it. But I saw it as a result of a crisis in Gothenburg. After the so-called generational shift, RF Gothenburg had been very active for a few years. They did more actions than any other local, they had the biggest membership, they had functioning working groups, they printed propaganda, they made great banners. It all went well until some of the central figures no longer were as active and claimed that the entire organization had become shit. They didn't understand that the organization was bigger than them.

In Stockholm, where I was, the situation was different. We never had that "mania" they were so proud of in Gothenburg. We were active at a sustainable level. For us, there was no crisis in RF. I encouraged all members, in all locals, to look beyond their immediate circle and to not only compare RF now to RF before, but also to compare RF to other groups. And compared to other groups, we were still one of the most active, maybe the most active in all of Sweden. We had at least one activity per week, whether it was putting up posters, organizing a film screening, giving a lecture, attending a protest, or doing an action. If you look at the activity reports we wrote, they were quite comprehensive until the very end.

Sure, the organization had changed. We had some middle-class members, which clashed with the very strong working-class identity of the early years, and the boundaries to other leftist groups weren't drawn as strictly as before. I understood that critique, but for me it wasn't reason enough to bury the entire organization.

The repression is often cited as the reason for the dissolution, but I don't think that's true. We didn't actually talk much about the repression. If it played a role, then it was indirectly: It made it more difficult to be active, which meant that there was less activity than before. I guess that's true.

The mood at the nationwide meeting where the dissolution was decided on wasn't great, of course. From Stockholm, almost everyone was against it, but all others were for it. We considered keeping the organization alive by ourselves, but we had some internal problems. Among the people who absolutely wanted to keep RF alive were some who hardly did anything and were quite unreliable. That bothered me. I was irritated by them suddenly presenting themselves as super activists. So, in the end, I made my peace with the dissolution. It might have been about time.

The dissolution was announced on Facebook. It was a very short post and no reasons were given.

Yes, that was a travesty. A catastrophe, really, when you consider how much some people had sacrificed for the organization: time, money, their health. Four lines on Facebook,

fucking hell! But there was a lot about the dissolution that wasn't right. We must not forget that we also had comrades in prison.

Two more voices regarding the dissolution:

1: The local in Gothenburg was quite hierarchical. We only really understood that later. They had leaders. Not officially, but in reality. New members were chosen quite randomly. I think the main criterion was that they said whatever the leaders wanted them to say, which meant that the quality of the members decreased. Some were only members because their friends were, they had little other motivation. For us in Stockholm, Gothenburg became more and more of a nuisance. They and their stupid central committee had to approve all decisions. They no longer contributed anything to the organization, but at the same time, they strangled everything that was antiauthoritarian and came from Stockholm. No surprise that this created friction.

2: But everyone had voted for the central committee.

1: But it was their motion.

2: Yes, but we from Stockholm also voted for it for different reasons. And in the beginning it served a purpose. Communication became more effective, for example. We never saw the central committee as a body that would allow individuals to rule over the locals but as a coordinating group that could make fast decisions when it was necessary. The name "central committee" was just a humorous reference to the Soviet Union. But later, after the dissolution, it became obvious that the Gothenburg local was indeed hierarchical, that one person had a lot of power, and that this person was behind everything concerning the dissolution. This is what people from Gothenburg have told us who had been manipulated by him. He was tired of RF, and so the entire organization had to die. A narcissist.

1: Yes, and all that we only got to know later.

2: The motion was presented at a nationwide meeting in Stockholm.

1: But it was filed earlier.

1: But not much. That, however, was fine. You could file a motion until the meeting started. But while we thought, "Okay, this has to be discussed thoroughly," they wanted to decide right away, even before the official meeting kicked off. The argument was that if the motion passed, there was no need for a meeting anymore. This is not how it's supposed to work! We also wanted to discuss if Stockholm could carry on under the name Revolutionary Front by itself. But that fellow didn't want any such discussion. Besides, a new local was to be founded in Malmö …

1: But they were idiots, they also voted for the dissolution. He had brought them into RF, so of course they voted with him.

2: They had probably been manipulated too.

1: It was all shit, and all just because one person couldn't control his ego and didn't understand that he was getting in the way.

2: The dissolution wasn't done correctly. You can't just kill off a big and important political organization like that.

You must not allow one person to manipulate so many others. That really was a catastrophe. And then he even claimed a monopoly on the name! We weren't super strong in Stockholm, but in the last year or two before the dissolution we had more things going on than they did in Gothenburg. The worst part is this: Today, no one even goes near that guy, no one wants to have anything to do with him! Today, everyone knows that he's manipulative. Everything went downhill because one individual controlled all of Gothenburg.

1: That's what happens when you have a central committee and such crap.

2: We were part of the same organization and didn't become that way. It's a personal thing. He was a narcissist who attained a position of power.

1: Yes, but had the structure been different, he couldn't have attained that position. The more hierarchical the structure, the easier it is to turn authoritarian.

2: But in that sense, RF was always an authoritarian organization, never a network.

1: Not a network, but no authoritarian organization.

2: All organizations have leadership and therefore a certain level of authority. There are always some who have more influence than others. That's why we had the Operative Units. There were people who only wanted to fight, and people who wanted to get organized.

But is every organization authoritarian only because some are more active than others?

2: Okay, wrong choice of words maybe. Not authoritarian then, but there are leaders in most autonomous groups. They can have a positive or a negative effect on the group. I'm not arguing for authoritarianism, and if you see it your way, RF wasn't authoritarian. In Stockholm, for example, we changed the central committee representative every fourth month or so.

But the Stockholm local was always more anarchist?

2: That's right. But we were a united organization, with the same slogans on May 1, common leaflets, and shared finances. Public statements were made by the entire organization.

1: In the beginning that worked well. But the more hierarchical the organization became, the more this became a handicap.

2: Yes, it turned into a handicap—if that's the word you want to use.

1: Okay, a disability.

2: Yes! It became a problem for us that individual members could steer the organization in a certain direction. We dissolved because individuals in Gothenburg managed to determine the vote of their local and even of other locals. There are also members from Gothenburg and Örebro who today regret the dissolution. We were an autonomous organization, and then such a fascist loser comes along and thinks he can decide everything by himself, even claim the name! We had filed a motion of our own, demanding that, given all the repression, we'd focus on building a strong organizational structure for a while. We didn't have to be on the streets all the time. When RF was dissolved, the name RF alone kept the Nazis at bay. They weren't afraid of AFA, but they were certainly afraid of RF. But our motion was rejected.

I will not comment on the statements made in this chapter; they speak for themselves. But we can draw a few conclusions from these interviews:

1. All former members are proud of having been in RF.

2. All recall positive and negative aspects of the organization.

3. Most of them believe that the dissolution of RF has left a void in Sweden's autonomous left, which, so far, has not been filled by any other group.

FINAL REMARKS

RF grew from a group of five friends to a nationwide organization with several locals. Its members did much political work, and the name of the organization became infamous within the Swedish left, among the fascists, and in bourgeois media. RF is also well known among antifascist activists outside of Sweden.

There are many more stories from former members than the ones told in this book. Each member has their own memories from the organization. But the work on this book also brought commonalities to the surface: a strong collective identity, the view of fascists as class traitors, and the critique of an autonomous left that often had no place for working-class people.

For many RF members, the organization seemed to offer the only possibility to get organized politically. Many had the feeling of not fitting in with other leftist groups. RF's members were, for the most part, very young when they joined the organization, but they managed to build a form of organization that had never existed within the Swedish left. They proved that autonomous leftist politics were possible without a subculture. They considered the rest of the political scene elitist, consisting of people for whom personal fulfillment was more important than politics.

The mainstream image of RF still focuses on the violence and the militant antifascism. To some degree, RF bears responsibility for this. The organization never made much of an effort to be perceived in any other way. The left has used RF's reputation to shield itself against the criticism it received from RF. But RF was

about more than just violence. RF put class politics on the agenda of the autonomous left, and the organization reached people who otherwise would not have been interested in political organizing.

I might be wrong, but working on this book gave me the impression that the autonomous left could have gained a lot by taking RF and RF's criticism of it seriously. This could have made united, uncompromising class struggle possible.

Former members have stressed repeatedly in this book that although they were able to chase the Nazis out of the streets in the early 2000s, the current fascist threat is as big, if not bigger. The Sweden Democrats—sharing the same roots as the National Democrats whom RF fought on the streets of Sweden—are today the country's second strongest party, and the current center-right government is dependent on their support. It is clear that their political orientation has not changed, even if the party has been able to enter the corridors of power. It suffices to look at the endless list of racist and antiworker statements by its members, or at the motions they have filed in parliament, or at the laws they have helped pass. The latter could not have been done without the help of the bourgeois parties, of course. It seems to be true that "history teaches us that we haven't learned anything from history."

ACKNOWLEDGMENTS

I want to thank all the people who, in whatever way, have helped this book become a reality. Thanks to everyone for feedback and for providing material! Thanks to everyone who has helped with practical stuff! And thanks to everyone who kept on asking when the book would finally be done!

A special thanks to all who took the time to be interviewed!

NOTES

Translator's Preface to the English Edition

1 The website has been taken down, but substantial parts of it can be retrieved at www.web.archive.org.

Introduction

1 The "autonomous left" is used as an umbrella term in most western and northern European countries for left-wing activists and groups that are independent from political parties.

2 In 2014, RF members were featured in the VICE News program "The Rise of Sweden's Far-Left Militants," posted May 27, 2014, on YouTube. In 2013, a member of RF Örebro spoke with the Örebro daily *Nerikes Allehanda*.

The Beginnings

1 Revolutionär Kommunistisk Ungdom (Revolutionary Communist Youth) is the youth organization of the Communist Party; Ung Vänster (Young Left) is the youth organization of the Left Party; SUF stands for Syndikalistiskt Ungdomsförbund (Syndicalist Youth League), an independent organization close to the syndicalist union SAC (Sveriges Arbetares Centralorganisation); AFA stands for Antifascistisk Aktion, an independent network that will be mentioned often in this book.

2 "Suburbs" (*förorter*) in the Swedish context resemble French *banlieues*, not US suburbs. Most of them are home to socially disadvantaged communities, often with migrant backgrounds.

3 During an EU summit in Gothenburg in June 2001, there were big demonstrations and clashes between protesters and the police. Nineteen-year-old Hannes Westberg was shot by police in connection with a Reclaim the Streets event. It was the first time since 1931 that Swedish police opened fire on protesters.

4 Nationalsocialistiska Fronten; existed from 1994 to 2008.

5 GAIS (Göteborgs Atlet- och Idrottssällskap) and IFK Göteborg (Idrottsföreningen Kamraterna Göteborg) are, next to BK Häcken and Örgryte IS, the biggest football clubs in Gothenburg.

6 Örgryte IS; see note 5 above.

The Helipad

1 The helipad, which was built into the waterways near the old town of Stockholm, was a legendary meeting place for right-wing skinheads. It will be referenced in this book frequently. The helipad was demolished in 2018.

2 The Sweden Democrats (Sverigedemokraterna) were founded in 1988 in Sweden's far-right/neo-Nazi milieu. In 2022, they received the second-most votes in the Swedish parliament elections with 21 percent, beaten only by the Social Democrats.

3 Engelbrekt Engelbrektsson was the leader of the so-called Engelbrekt Rebellion in 1434 against the Danish King Eric of Pomerania, who at the time also ruled over Sweden. Charles XII was king of Sweden from 1697 to 1718 and the last ruler of the "Swedish Empire" that stretched across vast parts of northern Europe. Their respective days of death, April 27 and November 30, are commemorated by events held by the far right. In 2023, the Sweden Democrats filed a motion in the Swedish parliament to replace May 1 as a national holiday with the Engelbrekt Day.

4 Info-14 was a far-right network that existed around a journal of the same name, published from 1995 to 2011 (from 2000 on as an online journal).

5 AIK (Allmänna Idrottsklubben) and Djurgården IF are, next to Hammarby IF, the biggest football clubs in Stockholm.

6 Kickers are a Swedish youth culture that emerged in the 1990s: athletic brands, electronic music, butterfly knives. Related to British casuals (see note 9 below).

7 Ingen människa är illegal is a Swedish migrant justice network, related to networks with the same name in other countries.

8 With regard to the events of that day, see also the memory "For us, this is nothing new, but many of them realize for the first time in their lives that the cops will never be on our side" (pp. 80–82).

9 Casuals are a British subculture that emerged in the late 1970s; in short, hooligans in designer clothes.

10 Since 2014, Kinnunen has served as an MP for the Sweden Democrats.

11 Since 2014, Sjöstedt has served as an MP for the Sweden Democrats.

12 *Under det rosa täcket* (Under the pink blanket) by Nina Björk, released in 1996, had big influence on feminist debate in Sweden.

13 From 2006 to 2014, Fredrik Reinfeldt (Moderate Party) served as prime minister of a center-right government coalition. (For the Moderate Party, see note 9 in "Direction: Change.")

"We Are 18.6"

1 A special section on the far-right Salem March, which was held annually from 2001 to 2012, appears on pp. 94–98.

2 June 6 is the Swedish National Day. On June 6, 1523, Gustav Vasa was crowned King of Sweden. Far-right groups commonly organize rallies on that day.

3 In Swedish, Göteborgs Fria Nationalister.

4 Nätverket mot rasism was a network of different left-wing and antiracist groups and organizations that existed from 1995 to 2010.

5 Frihetliga fotbollscupen was a football tournament for left-wing teams held in Stockholm from 1990 to 2010.
6 Kafé 44 is a legendary meeting place and venue of the autonomous left and punk scene in Stockholm.
7 "Little League" is a translation of the Swedish *Knatteligan*, which includes wordplay that cannot be reproduced in English: *Knatteligan* is, on one hand, a sports league for young children (*knatte*), but *liga* is also a Swedish term for "gang."
8 In the 1970s and '80s, thousands of left-wing refugees came from Latin America to Sweden, especially from Chile. They were fleeing the military dictatorships there.
9 "Home visits" refers in this context to harassing or attacking political activists at their places of residence.
10 For AIK, see note 5 in "The Helipad."
11 "Violent capital" (*våldskapital*) is a term used in Swedish in connection with gang violence but also militant political groups. It refers to the level of violence that groups are willing and able to use, and the (real or imagined) danger that implies. The term was translated in this book in different ways—for example, "readiness to use violence" or "level of violence"—depending on context.
12 Sergels Torg is a square in central Stockholm adjacent to the central railway station. Many political rallies are held there.

"Our Mere Existence Posed a Threat to Them"

1 Red Action was a militant socialist and antifascist network in the UK, active from 1980 to 2000.
2 Yelah was an online portal of the autonomous left that existed from 1994 to 2015. *ETC* is the biggest left-wing daily in Sweden.
3 In July 1908, striking workers planted a bomb on the ship *Amalthea* in the harbor of Malmö. *Amalthea* housed workers from England used as strikebreakers; one of them, Walter Close, died in the attack. The event is an important reference point for the Swedish left.
4 Nordiska Motståndsrörelsen (Nordic Resistance Movement), a neo-Nazi network founded in 1997 with chapters in Sweden, Norway, Finland, and Denmark. The Swedish chapter is the biggest.
5 SAC stands for Sveriges Arbetares Centralorganisation (Central Organization of Workers in Sweden), a federation of local syndicalist unions founded in 1910.
6 Huvudstadens Södra Kommando; for more on the Operative Units, see the section starting on p. 114.
7 For kickers, see note 6 in "The Helipad."
8 In Sweden, the term *bourgeois* is commonly used for center-right politics (essentially, everything between social democracy and the far right).
9 Busslink is a Swedish bus company that RF targeted in a campaign protesting poor working conditions. Annie Lööf was the chairwoman of the neoliberal Center Party from 2011 to 2023. From 2011 to 2014, she served as minister of economy in the center-right coalition led by Fredrik Reinfeldt; for Reinfeldt, see note 13 in "The Helipad."

10 Varis is an antifascist network in Finland founded in 2014.
11 *No Retreat: The Secret War Between Britain's Anti-Fascists and the Far Right* by Dave Hann and Steve Tilzey was published in 2003 by Milo Books. For Red Action, see note 1 in this chapter.
12 Former IRA member; imprisoned 1973–1980 and 2011–2013.
13 For Kafé 44, see note 6 in "We Are 18.6."
14 Arbetarnas Bildningsförbund (Workers' Educational Association). Founded in 1912, ABF focuses on educational programs for adults; the organization is closely tied to the Social Democratic Party and has hundreds of locals in all parts of Sweden.
15 Systembolaget is a Swedish state company with a monopoly on selling alcohol.

RF Gains Territory

1 The incident is also referred to in the interview "We Came from the Streets, We Didn't Need to Go There" (pp. 11–22).
2 There were similar groups in other European countries, for example the Autonomen Nationalisten in Germany. These groups followed traditional far-right ideology but stressed the importance of local, independent organizing. Today, they have lost nearly all significance, although traces can be found in the Identitarian Movement and similar "alt-right" tendencies.
3 Solna Torg is a square in the municipality of Solna, located in the north of the greater Stockholm metropolitan area.
4 A section dedicated to the Salem March appears on pp. 94–98. The Yellow Cross (Gula Korset) was a prisoner support group connected to Info-14. For Info-14, see note 4 in "The Helipad."
5 A municipality in the southern part of the greater Stockholm metropolitan area.
6 The Royal Gardens (Kungsträdgården) lie near the Royal Castle in the center of Stockholm; in 2014, antifascist protesters clashed there with police during a rally of the Party of the Swedes. In the Stockholm suburb of Kärrtorp, an antifascist manifestation was attacked by NMR members in December 2013 (see the section "Kärrtorp, Operation Eskil, and Repression" on pp. 171–73). In the town of Limhamn, in the south of Sweden, antifascists clashed with police in August 2014, also during a rally of the Party of the Swedes.
7 A leading figure in Info-14.
8 In Swedish, *Salemfacklan*.

No Class, Only Style

1 *Aftonbladet* is a social democratic tabloid and one of the biggest Swedish dailies. Mona Sahlin was the chairwoman of the Social Democratic Party from 2007 to 2011.
2 Sweden had a relatively large number of Nazi sympathizers during the Third Reich.
3 *Jobbjakt* literally means "job hunt."
4 *Badvakt*, literally "bath guard."
5 In September 2012, RF attacked a far-right festival in the town of Kolsva, located between Örebro and Västerås.

Linköping and More About the Operative Units

1 Gösta Hallberg-Cuula was a Swedish Nazi leader who perished as a volunteer with Finnish forces fighting the Soviet Red Army in 1942.
2 For the Swedish National Day, see note 2 in "We Are 18.6."

Örebro and More About Home Visits

1 A street in Eskilstuna.

Direction: Change

1 In Swedish, Svenskarnas Parti.
2 SMR stands for Svenska Motståndsrörelsen (Swedish Resistance Movement), the Swedish chapter of NMR. Since 2016, NMR no longer uses the names of the national chapters officially.
3 Skåne is Sweden's southernmost region, known also to English speakers as Scania.
4 Nordisk Ungdom (Nordic Youth) was a far-right network that existed from 2010 to 2019. *Querfront* (literally "cross front") is a German term stemming from the 1930s that signifies attempts to bring together far-right and far-left forces.
5 On June 6, 2009 (Swedish National Day), the Sweden Democrat Martin Kinnunen and his partner were attacked and injured by three women at the Gullmarsplan subway station in Stockholm. The three women received prison sentences from nine to eighteen months. On Kinnunen, see also p. 22 and note 10 in "The Helipad."
6 Backaplan is a shopping mall in northern Gothenburg.
7 *Uppdrag Granskning* is a popular investigative Swedish TV program focusing on sociopolitical issues. The episode on RF aired in May 2014.
8 Aktion mot Deportation, a network focusing on refugee aid and resistance to deportations in the 2010s.
9 The Moderate Party (Moderaterna) is the biggest bourgeois party in Sweden. The current (June 2025) prime minister of Sweden, Ulf Kristersson, comes from the party; he leads a center-right coalition supported by the Sweden Democrats.
10 The Swedish school system contains several divisions. Primary and secondary schools are attended by students from the age of six to fifteen. High schools are attended from the age of fifteen to eighteen.
11 Even when schools are privately run in Sweden, they receive government subsidies.
12 In Swedish, Förbundet Nationell Ungdom.
13 For SMR, see note 2 in this chapter.
14 Ronny and Ragge are fictitious characters representing the Swedish *raggare* subculture—old American cars, rockabilly, partying—popular in the Swedish countryside. In the 1990s, Ronny and Ragge had their own TV show and released several records.

Malmö and More About the Macho Critique

1 Feminist group in Malmö.

2 A town in the south of Sweden, located between Malmö and Gothenburg; RF's last local was formed there (see p. 166).
3 With Collective Effort, there has been a popular left-wing sports club in Malmö since 2017.
4 In the Stockholm suburb of Kärrtorp, a far-right attack on an antifascist manifestation occurred in December 2013. On March 8, 2014, antifascists in Malmö received life-threatening injuries during a confrontation with members of the Party of the Swedes. More on these events below.
5 For SMR, see note 2 in "Direction: Change."
6 The prominent left-wing activist and football supporter Showan Shattak received life-threatening injuries that day.

The Repression Is Taking a Toll

1 For SMR, see note 2 in "Direction: Change."
2 For *Aftonbladet*, see note 1 in "No Class, Only Style."

The End

1 Djurrättsalliansen, an animal rights organization founded in 2005.
2 For *Uppdrag Granskning*, see note 7 in "Direction: Change."

ABOUT THE CONTRIBUTORS

Emma Hagberg is an activist, writer, and educator from Stockholm, Sweden, with years of experience in the extraparliamentary left. She has worked on a range of subjects, from the anarchist movement in Greece to antifascist mobilization in the Nordic countries. She lives in Stockholm. Emma welcomes feedback to the book. You can reach her at belpublishing@proton.me or via Instagram at @bel.publishing.

Gabriel Kuhn is an Austrian-born writer and translator living in Sweden. He has authored and translated more than twenty books, many with PM Press.

Tomas Rothaus is a lifelong anarchist and antifascist as well as an athlete and a father. PM Press published his first three books, *Another War Is Possible*; *Argentina, a Tale of Two Utopias*; and *From Riot to Insurrection*.

ABOUT PM PRESS

PM Press is an independent, radical publisher of critically necessary books for our tumultuous times. Our aim is to deliver bold political ideas and vital stories to all walks of life and arm the dreamers to demand the impossible. Founded in 2007 by a small group of people with decades of publishing, media, and organizing experience, we have sold millions of copies of our books, most often one at a time, face to face. We're old enough to know what we're doing and young enough to know what's at stake. Join us to create a better world.

PM Press
PO Box 23912
Oakland, CA 94623
www.pmpress.org

PM Press in Europe
europe@pmpress.org
www.pmpress.org.uk

FRIENDS OF PM PRESS

These are indisputably momentous times—the financial system is melting down globally and the Empire is stumbling. Now more than ever there is a vital need for radical ideas.

In the many years since its founding—and on a mere shoestring—PM Press has risen to the formidable challenge of publishing and distributing knowledge and entertainment for the struggles ahead. With hundreds of releases to date, we have published an impressive and stimulating array of literature, art, music, politics, and culture. Using every available medium, we've succeeded in connecting those hungry for ideas and information to those putting them into practice.

Friends of PM allows you to directly help impact, amplify, and revitalize the discourse and actions of radical writers, filmmakers, and artists. It provides us with a stable foundation from which we can build upon our early successes and provides a much-needed subsidy for the materials that can't necessarily pay their own way. You can help make that happen—and receive every new title automatically delivered to your door once a month—by joining as a Friend of PM Press. And, we'll throw in a free T-shirt when you sign up.

Here are your options:

- **$30 a month** Get all books and pamphlets plus a 50% discount on all webstore purchases
- **$40 a month** Get all PM Press releases (including CDs and DVDs) plus a 50% discount on all webstore purchases
- **$100 a month** Superstar—Everything plus PM merchandise, free downloads, and a 50% discount on all webstore purchases

For those who can't afford $30 or more a month, we have **Sustainer Rates** at $15, $10 and $5. Sustainers get a free PM Press T-shirt and a 50% discount on all purchases from our website.

Your Visa or Mastercard will be billed once a month, until you tell us to stop. Or until our efforts succeed in bringing the revolution around. Or the financial meltdown of Capital makes plastic redundant. Whichever comes first.

ABOUT US

Working Class History is an international collective of worker-activists focused on the research and promotion of people's history through our podcasts, websites, books, and social media channels.

We want to uncover stories of our collective history of fighting for better world and tell them in a straightforward and engaging way to help educate and inspire new generations of activists.

Through our social media outlets with over two million followers, we reach an audience of over 20 million per month. So if you're on social media, you can connect with us in the following ways:

- Website: workingclasshistory.com
- Instagram: @workingclasshistory
- Facebook: facebook.com/workingclasshistory
- Twitter: @wrkclasshistory
- YouTube: youtube.com/workingclasshistory
- Mastodon: mastodon.social/@workingclasshistory
- Bluesky: @workingclasshistory.com

We receive no funding from any political party, academic institution, corporation or government. All of our work is funded entirely by our readers and listeners on patreon. So if you appreciate what we do, consider joining us, supporting our work and getting access exclusive content and benefits at patreon.com/workingclasshistory.

Antifascism, Sports, Sobriety: Forging a Militant Working-Class Culture

Julius Deutsch
Edited and translated by Gabriel Kuhn

ISBN: 978-1-62963-154-7
$14.95 128 pages

The Austromarxist era of the 1920s was a unique chapter in socialist history. Trying to carve out a road between reformism and Bolshevism, the Austromarxists embarked on an ambitious journey towards a socialist oasis in the midst of capitalism. Their showpiece, the legendary "Red Vienna," has worked as a model for socialist urban planning ever since.

At the heart of the Austromarxist experiment was the conviction that a socialist revolution had to entail a cultural one. Numerous workers' institutions and organizations were founded, from education centers to theaters to hiking associations. With the Fascist threat increasing, the physical aspects of the cultural revolution became ever more central as they were considered mandatory for effective defense. At no other time in socialist history did armed struggle, sports, and sobriety become as intertwined in a proletarian attempt to protect socialist achievements as they did in Austria in the early 1930s. Despite the final defeat of the workers' militias in the Austrian Civil War of 1934 and subsequent Fascist rule, the Austromarxist struggle holds important lessons for socialist theory and practice.

Antifascism, Sports, Sobriety contains an introductory essay by Gabriel Kuhn and selected writings by Julius Deutsch, leader of the workers' militias, president of the Socialist Workers' Sport International, and a prominent spokesperson for the Austrian workers' temperance movement. Deutsch represented the physical defense of the working class against its enemies like few others. His texts in this book are being made available in English for the first time.

"An almost completely forgotten episode in labor history."
—Murray Bookchin, author of *Anarchism, Marxism and the Future of the Left*

"A foretaste of the socialist utopia of the future in the present."
—Helmut Gruber, author of *Red Vienna: Experiment in Working-Class Culture, 1919–1934*

"The insurrection of February 1934 . . . left behind the glorious memory of resistance to fascism by arms and not merely by speeches."
—E.J. Hobsbawm, author of *The Age of Extremes: The Short Twentieth Century, 1914–1991*

Antifascistas: Resisting Spain's Far Right

Miquel Ramos with a Foreword by Tomas Rothaus

ISBN: 979-8-88744-218-1
$25.95 480 pages

This is a history of resistance that exposes how fascism adapts and how antifascism survives, learns, and fights back.

In Spain, the "transition" refers to the official passage from Franco's dictatorship to parliamentary monarchy after 1975. But while democracy was being declared, the far right was regrouping. Old Francoism mutated into vigilante squads, state terror networks, neo-Nazi skinhead gangs, soccer ultras, and eventually new neofascist movements determined to claw their way into public life and state institutions.

A generation of antifascists came of age in the shadow of this violence. Faced with attacks on immigrants, dissidents, and anyone deemed disposable, they organized across neighborhoods, subcultures, and movements, refusing to accept the far right's return as inevitable.

Drawing on firsthand testimonies, investigative reporting, and political and historical accounts, Ramos traces the antifascist struggle in Spain from the mid-1980s to the present. He documents how diverse individuals and collectives confronted neofascist forces, moving from urgent self-defense to coordinated offensive action. *Antifascistas* maps the crucial roles played by journalism, music, culture, institutions, and allied social movements, while reckoning honestly with internal debates, strategic failures, and hard-won victories.

"*Miquel Ramos is not only the leading journalist of antifascist and far-right politics in Spain but also a longtime militant who has lived much of the history he chronicles in his magnum opus,* Antifascistas. *Finally translated into English,* Antifascistas *crafts a rich and extensive tapestry of the continuation of the antifascist struggle in Spanish side streets and barrios after the death of Franco. An instant classic, Ramos's study is a compelling tale of everyday resistance and the first history of turn-of-twenty-first-century antifascism in Spain.*"
—Mark Bray, author of *Antifa: The Anti-Fascist Handbook*

"Antifascistas *presents a unique perspective on the militant struggle against the far right in Spain. The book combines historical accounts of fascist organizing and violence from the 1960s to the present with firsthand accounts of efforts to combat fascism. In telling this story, Ramos shows the international links of both fascist and antifascist movements and analyzes how subculture is a point of conflict between these two ideologies. This is an insightful read for anyone interested in the history and internal dynamics of contemporary antifascist struggle.*"
—Stanislav Vysotsky, author of *American Antifa: The Tactics, Practice, and Culture of Militant Antifascism*

Argentina, A Tale of Two Utopias: Anarchism, Soccer, Neoliberalism

Tomas Rothaus
with a Foreword by Gabriel Kuhn

ISBN: 979-8-88744-147-4
$22.95 304 pages

A Tale of Two Utopias takes us through the outsized and unexpected remnants of the influence of anarchist ideas and practice on modern-day Argentina—from the names of popular pastries to the foundation of numerous soccer clubs—until we arrive at the explosive intersection of anarchism, football, and the crisis of neoliberalism.

This is a thrilling first-person account of the December 2001 uprising in Argentina that marked the end of the neoliberal experiment of the 1990s, narrated by an anarchist participant in the clashes that laid siege to the presidential palace and forced the president to resign and flee on a rooftop helicopter. *A Tale of Two Utopias* weaves together two simultaneous yet seemingly unrelated events of those "days which contain decades" of Buenos Aires in December 2001: the uprising and the first championship in 35 years of the popular football club Racing Club de Avellaneda.

Alternating between urgent narration and historical account, and accompanied by over 150 photos and illustrations, *A Tale of Two Utopias* has the reader walking the streets of a Buenos Aires on fire, while finding the time to take us on a lovingly traced tour of the rich history of Argentina's anarchist movement of the early twentieth century (then among the largest in the world)—and it is also a compelling account of the trauma inflicted by Argentina's numerous dictatorships.

"A Tale of Two Utopias *weaves complicated histories of anarchism, football, resistance, and everyday life in Buenos Aires into an artful narrative of youthful exuberance and political turmoil. As opposition boils up again today in Argentina, this riveting snapshot of popular outrage from below presents readers with a fascinating point of inflection to connect general strikes and dreams of revolution, past and present.*"
—Mark Bray, author of *Antifa: The Anti-Fascist Handbook*

We Go Where They Go: The Story of Anti-Racist Action

Shannon Clay, Lady, Kristin Schwartz, and Michael Staudenmaier with a Foreword by Gord Hill

ISBN: 978-1-62963-972-7 (paperback)
978-1-62963-977-2 (hardcover)
$24.95/$59.95 320 pages

What does it mean to risk all for your beliefs? How do you fight an enemy in your midst? *We Go Where They Go* recounts the thrilling story of a massive forgotten youth movement that set the stage for today's antifascist organizing in North America. When skinheads and punks in the late 1980s found their communities invaded by white supremacists and neo-nazis, they fought back. Influenced by anarchism, feminism, Black liberation, and Indigenous sovereignty, they created Anti-Racist Action. At ARA's height in the 1990s, thousands of dedicated activists in hundreds of chapters joined the fights—political and sometimes physical—against nazis, the Ku Klux Klan, antiabortion fundamentalists, and racist police. Before media pundits, cynical politicians, and your uncle discovered "antifa," Anti-Racist Action was bringing it to the streets.

Based on extensive interviews with dozens of ARA participants, *We Go Where They Go* tells ARA's story from within, giving voice to those who risked their safety in their own defense and in solidarity with others. In reproducing the posters, zines, propaganda, and photos of the movement itself, this essential work of radical history illustrates how cultural scenes can become powerful forces for change. Here at last is the story of an organic yet highly organized movement, exploring both its triumphs and failures, and offering valuable lessons for today's generation of activists and rabble-rousers. *We Go Where They Go* is a page-turning history of grassroots antiracism. More than just inspiration, it's a roadmap.

"I was a big supporter and it was an honor to work with the Anti-Racist Action movement. Their unapologetic and uncompromising opposition to racism and fascism in the streets, in the government, and in the mosh pit continues to be inspiring to this day."
—Tom Morello

"Antifa became a household word with Trump attempting and failing to designate it a domestic terrorist group, but Antifa's roots date back to the late 1980s when little attention was being paid to violent fascist groups that were flourishing under Reaganism, and Anti-Racist Action (ARA) was singular and effective in its brilliant offensive. This book tells the story of ARA in breathtaking prose accompanied by stunning photographs and images."
—Roxanne Dunbar-Ortiz, author of *Loaded: A Disarming History of the Second Amendment*